ROAD STORIES

ED DAVIS

ISBN: 098606971X
ISBN-13: 9780986069710
Library of Congress Control Number: 2013919216
CreateSpace Independent Publishing Platform
North Charleston, South Carolina

For Jan

Contents

FORWARD

We spend our lives on the road. We may never leave our hometown or never find one, but from that first trip home in our mother's arms to wherever our final journey takes us we are always traveling. The people we come to know and places we visit, even in passing, shape who we become and inform who we are.

Even standing still, in our minds we are always moving; though memories of things seen and done, through planned excursions yet to come, through fantasy adventures that may never be. Our best and oldest stories are about travel, going all the way back to legend. All of us are on our own hero's journey.

There is travel we require to sustain our lives, and travel we require to enrich them. They can be one and the same. Twilight holds magic, whether seen from a mountaintop or a traffic jam. The wisdom of the neighbor next door is no less profound than the words of a Lama a continent away. Yet familiarity can blur our vision, and nothing helps us focus like the unknown.

So we strike out, senses heightened and expectations high, to see what awaits us around the next bend, and what we may discover about ourselves when we get there.

Ed Davis
June 2, 2013
Glen Ellen, California

Ganges

British Columbia

August, 1972

It was a sweet, cool, still sort of a night; peaceful and warm in the way Canadian summer nights can be. The air was fragrant with smells of earth and forest, and the wind carried the unmistakable scent of the nearby sea. A full moon cast a pale glow, turning the beautifully wooded nearby hills into a ghostly shadow world that bore almost no resemblance to what I'd seen in the light of day.

I watched the whole silent landscape from the porch of Sarah's second story apartment in the middle of Ganges. She lived with three other girls in the ramshackle old place situated directly above the Gulf Islands Trading Company. The Trading Company served as a sort of Sears and Roebuck for the whole string of Gulf Islands, supplying, at no small price, most anything that one might need. When Sarah first arrived in the islands she'd worked there in the meat department. Being an employee, the Trading Company gave her special consideration and rented her the rundown flat upstairs at a reduced rate. Within a week of moving in she got disgusted with overcharging people and quit her job. But she didn't move out, much to the displeasure of the Trading Company management. And she won't until she's damn good and ready.

This was the first night Paul and I stayed on Salt Spring Island, and the first night we'd had a chance to sleep anywhere but under the stars or in a freight car since leaving home. Sarah had invited us to stay at her place, have a home cooked meal and sleep out of the weather for once. She didn't know us, she didn't owe us anything, but she didn't work that way. We must have looked friendly enough, sitting with our backpacks on the porch of the Trading Company, sharing some Canadian beer. We obviously needed a place to stay. It was just that simple.

Everyone in the house had gone to bed; Paul and I were on floor mattresses in the front room. We had traveled a long way that day, and by rights should have crashed immediately, but I couldn't. Try as I might there was no way I could clear my head of thoughts about the trip; the rides we'd gotten, decisions we'd made, people we'd met; and most of all, where we were headed next. Paul and I planned to cross Canada separately; Ganges was where we'd be splitting up.

Restless, I pulled on my Levi's. The house was very old, with creaky boards under the faded linoleum, so I tiptoed out onto the large open porch that ran the length of the building. There were sagging clotheslines criss-crossing over it, and a few broken wicker chairs off in a corner. A waist-high railing ran around the sides, and it was on this railing that I chose to sit, dangling my legs out over the street and taking in the whole night scene. From my perch I could see the entire center of the small town, and anyone who passed there. It was like looking through a two-way mirror; I was able to observe people on the street below, but unless they happened to glance up they would never see me.

Surprisingly there were lots of folks out in Ganges at that hour, though it was nearly midnight. There weren't crowds, but people did come by fairly often, maybe on their way home from the pub or just out for a late walk. As they strolled by, sometimes passing right beneath me, I was able to see them in a way that I hadn't before. They didn't know they were being observed, they were not the least bit nervous or ill at ease, and since there was no reason to act otherwise they were totally natural.

As I watched, I began to silently describe the people that I saw, to look closely at every movement and feature and to construct verbal pictures of them in my mind. Soon I was not only taking note of their physical characteristics, but also of what I thought their mood might be. I started making up whole histories for the people as they passed, guessing at the events that led them to the main street of Ganges late on that summer night. It was a challenge, and it was fun. I sat there in the moonlight, wearing nothing but my Levi's, and watched people, really watched them, until no more people came.

What prompted me to look so differently at people on that particular moonlit night, in that particular place? My secret observation post must have had something to do with it, but whatever the reason my outlook seemed to change permanently. I found myself thinking about strangers whom I normally would not have noticed at all; old men with wine bottles, young lovers on a stroll, bus drivers, store clerks, cops; anyone who caught my eye and looked interesting, which was almost everyone.

I finally went to sleep that night, with a head full of words to write about what I'd seen on the street. Next morning the words were mostly gone, but the desire to write them wasn't. On the rest of that trip and on many since, anytime my freight got sidelined or a ride wouldn't come, or I just had a few minutes to spare, I would often find myself writing as I waited; capturing as best I could the beats and rhythms of the road and the people I met upon it.

Gastown

British Columbia

August 1972

A paddy wagon was slowly working its way down the block towards where we sat on the cold stone benches of Pigeon Park. Two big Indian kids had passed out on the sidewalk up there and the cops were having some difficulty waking them up to arrest them. They were really big kids, three hundred pounders at least, so the cops couldn't possibly have gotten them into the paddy wagon without a crane. We watched with interest and more than a little amusement as the cops would struggle to wake up one of the massive drunks, only to have him pass out again before he could rise to his feet. Then they'd try the other one, with no better success. Then back to the first.

Louise, on the bench next to me, was really into it, really showing some signs of life for the first time in the several hours we'd been friends, if friends is the right word. All we'd actually done was share the same marble bench through the small hours of the morning, and after she'd become accustomed to me, we'd shared her newly opened bottle of cheap sherry. From the moment she came and sat down beside me I don't think we said more than a dozen words to each other. She just huddled there on the bench; small and ghostlike in her long gray overcoat, and only moving to avoid getting stepped on by the weaving drunks and prostitutes that came staggering by.

Everything about her looked ancient; the broken down shoes, the short-cropped white hair so thin it barely covered her scalp. Her whole body was bent and gnarled; twisted, probably diseased, hopelessly old. Whenever a whore came strutting by with an eager client on her arm Louise would lift her gaze and with a look of contempt watch the couple until they disappeared back into the crowd. I suspect she may have been a prostitute once herself. She didn't actually tell me that or anything else much. She talked almost constantly, but to the street, not to me.

The two of us sitting on that bench had to have looked strange to the night people as they shuffled by. As strange, I guess, as anything can in downtown Vancouver at four o'clock in the morning. The regulars must have wondered what Grandma Louise, the matron of Gastown, was doing with that big bearded stranger by her side. And what's more, she was sharing her precious sherry with him. How long, I wonder, had they seen the old lady sitting there in Pigeon Park or maybe up the street at Victory Square, sitting with the ever present bottle tucked safely beneath her tattered gray coat and casting a steely-eyed challenge at anyone who came near and looked thirsty? How many nights had the winos and Indians and whores down there wanted to jump the old broad for her booze, and how many nights had they not? And now she was sharing it with me.

"Ah, you fuckin' cops, leave them boys alone!"

She was actually pretty easy to understand when she was screaming. Most of the night she'd just been mumbling to the street, and I hadn't understood more than a word or two. Now, at full volume, everyone for blocks caught her meaning, especially the cops up the street.

"They ain't bothering nobody, God damn it!" Then at half volume, "Them goddamned fuckin' cops." Then, increasing to a shriek again, "Why don't you go home where you belong and leave us decent folks in peace."

She took another pull from the bottle and handed it to me. "They're the ones making all the trouble around here, them fuckers." As she said the last word her voice trailed off into another mumbled monologue to the street.

An Indian we'd seen making the rounds earlier slithered up and sat down next to her on the far end of our bench. I say our bench because, after our long occupation it seemed like ours, at least to us. Intruders were not welcome, particularly intruders who looked as thirsty as this one. We'd see him hitting up tourists for spare change earlier in the evening when there were still tourists around. Then, as it got later and only the regular crowd was left on the streets, we'd watched him drift from group to group; wino to wino, trying anybody who looked like they might be hiding a drink.

Just before the cops arrived he and a couple of others had rolled an old man across the street from us and taken his wallet---literally just rolled him over because he was already falling down drunk---but apparently they came up empty. Finally, in desperation, he'd mustered the courage to come over and try taking the old lady's bottle, in spite of the fact that I, seemingly her friend, was sitting so near.

Louise immediately shied away and scooted towards my end of the bench. There was no fear in what she did, just anger and disgust at the creature that was about to attack her. Like a cat drawing itself up before a fight she sat tense and poised, tightly clutching the hidden sherry to her breast, willing to defend it at all costs. There was something impressive, almost noble, about her defiance, meek as it was.

The attack, however, barely came. What did come was the paddy wagon, whose drivers had taken Louise's advice and left the fat boys to lie in peace. As it pulled up to where we sat the intruder made a grab for Louise's bottle and tried to dash off, but she wasn't having it. There was a clumsy struggle for a few seconds before a young cop jumped from his seat and ended the whole affair. He snatched the bottle from amidst grasping hands and poured its whole precious contents out into the street.

The three of us raised our voices in protest, all united now against the injustice. The cop, who was clearly familiar with my bench mates, ignored them completely. His gaze rested uneasily on me.

"Them I know," he said. "What are you doing here?"

What, indeed.

A DOZEN HOURS earlier my hitched ride from the ferry terminal deposited me right in the middle of central Vancouver; the business district, complete with sky scrapers and the whole schmear, but without a trace of the freight yard I'd hoped to find before dark. Nearly an hour passed before I was able to locate anyone on that quiet afternoon that even thought they knew where the freights could be found. People seldom seem to know or even care about trains anymore, and that makes riding "economy class" even more difficult than it must have been back in Depression days.

I finally came across an old timer who thought I might have some luck down by Hastings Street, down near the river, "by that Gastown place," he said. So off I went, whistling down the long, sloping Vancouver streets and thinking of what lay ahead. Three thousand miles of Canada stretched invitingly out before me. All I had to do was catch a fast eastbound freight to see it all.

I found the yards just where the old guy said they'd be, but they were put together differently than any I'd ever seen before. Big city yards are usually wide, thirty or forty sidings worth, but not Vancouver. There were only a handful of tracks forming what almost looked like a tunnel running through, and sometimes actually under the close-set surrounding buildings. I didn't like the look of it. Sizing up and catching a freight takes room, and the prospect of confinement to that narrow slash through the city wasn't appealing at all. But neither was the prospect of a long walk back to the highway and hitch hiking.

I jumped down onto the tracks, asked a switchman where I might catch an eastbound, and headed off in the direction he indicated. As it turned out, the eastbound yard was situated directly behind the row of tenements that had so recently been transformed into Gastown.

My intention was to grab the first freight east, or even north, just so I wouldn't be faced with spending a night in the city. If you get stuck in some small town or out in the sticks it's easy to find an out-of-the-way place to tuck in for the night. A city is a completely different story, particularly if you don't have a pile of money to blow on a hotel room. I meant to snag the first train leaving, and just needed to find out where to catch it.

There were a surprising number of people down around the tracks there, but none of them railroad types who could tell me what I needed to know. Most were well dressed, most in a hurry. It didn't make any sense at all until I saw them making for a back entrance to Gastown. Things started to look up when a group of track workers, just off shift, came past. But one of them didn't like longhairs and started getting vocal about it. I stayed silent as they walked by.

It was getting late and my chances were fading with the daylight when I happened across an aging switch engineer. He was taking a leak between two parked cars on a side street next to the tracks. The old boomer could see immediately that I was looking for a train, and was pleased to tell me that he'd just finished making up an eastbound that was scheduled to pull out at eleven o'clock. His shift had just ended, he was heading into Gastown for a few drinks before going home, and he offered to show me a grocery store so I could stock up before the trip.

The back entrance to Gastown was just a break in some hurricane fence. As I followed him through it, the transition was instantaneous. Less than a hundred yards from where I'd just watched the guy peeing on somebody's tire, we were standing in what looked like Fisherman's Wharf on a Sunday afternoon in July. There were people everywhere; coming out of high-class restaurants, browsing at shop windows, listening and dancing to street band music. He showed me to a little health food store, full of just what I needed for the trip, and bid me farewell.

On the road I learned that it was easiest to carry lightweight, high protein food, so that's what I stocked up on; raisins, nuts, cheese, chocolate. The young Asian girl behind the counter gave me a great big smile and undercharged me for the groceries. How fine I felt walking back through those crowded streets, totally resolute on jumping that eleven o'clock freight and being in Calgary by sundown the following day.

Things were just as good down by the tracks. I plopped down on a loading dock that faced the yard; it turned out to be the service entrance for one of those fancy restaurants I'd seen. The place was called Brother John's, and its claim to fame was that all the waiters dressed like Friar Tuck. The friars would come out back on the landing for a break and a smoke, and I got friendly with one of them in particular. He was curious about traveling, I was curious about life as a waiter dressed as a friar. Before I knew it the big, six-engine eastbound started rolling past and it was time to go.

The freight couldn't have been moving at more than five miles per hour. I took my time hoisting my pack onto my shoulder and bidding farewell to the friendly waiter. It was just like the scene at the end of Picnic where William Holden leaves Kim Novak and catches a freight for Tulsa, waiving from atop a boxcar with the setting sun in the background. Not exactly like it you understand; no Kim Novak and no setting sun, but still similar enough to make me feel like the real deal. I swaggered up next to that big slow freight and waited for the right car to come by.

It was then that my movie started falling apart.

William Holden caught a boxcar on his train and I intended to do the same. The night showed signs of getting pretty damn cold and I wanted to be out of the wind and weather at least until sunup. The problem was that no boxcars came rolling by at all. No boxcars, no gondolas, no refrigerator cars, no bulk feeders . . . nothing on the whole damn train but Pigs. Every last car on that entire two-mile long freight was a piggyback. They're good for carrying tractor-trailers, or autos on their way from the factory to the showroom, but they make for an absolutely miserable ride. There is no shelter from the wind, no place to hide from the bulls, and very little to hang on to.

So I just stood there, looking less and less like William Holden by the minute and watching the whole blessed freight pass by. Ironically, just as the caboose lights were fading in the distance I felt a tap on my shoulder. Who should it be but the old switch engineer I'd met earlier.

"Well boy, there went your ride."

"Yeah, the whole thing was pigs."

"Sorry I didn't mention that," he said, "wasn't thinking I guess. But don't let it get you down. There should be another one along about three in the morning, and it's sure to have some empties. 'I was you, I'd stash that big old pack somewhere and go kill time in a pub 'till the next one rolls out. Suit yourself though, and good luck to you."

Lacking a better idea, I tucked my pack safely away beneath an abandoned loading dock, straightened my hair a little, took beer money in hand and headed back through the fence to Gastown.

THE PUBS IN Vancouver, or all of Canada maybe, are not at all like American bars. They don't serve hard liquor, only beer. And you must be seated to drink; standing at the bar is prohibited. These beer parlors are big and well lit, places to share a drink and socialize rather than drown your sorrows in solitude.

I walked into just such an establishment and it was packed. After much maneuvering and scouting I found an empty chair at a small table near the back, and joined a well-dressed middle aged fellow already sitting there reading the evening paper. He smiled as I approached, the bar man brought around a couple of fresh glasses, and I settled in to enjoy my few hours' wait until the next train.

The gent at my table finished his paper and we started talking easily. I got a fair amount of his story and a pretty good tour of Gastown's nightspots before we parted company. He was partial to Yanks, and had pegged me as one even before I spoke. He'd been to the States once, a dozen years earlier, and though he lost his shirt gambling in Reno and had to hitch hike home, he had fond memories of the experience and a generous attitude towards anyone associated with it. Somehow that extended to me.

It turned out that he'd been waiting for his girlfriend to join him, but when she failed to show up we decided to make a night of it. We went to one pub after another; sharing sociable beers, checking out the girls, having a good old time. I wasn't really dressed for a night on the town, wearing my dirty road clothes and stocking cap, but it didn't seem to matter. He kept showing me around to the different clubs and burlesque houses like I was a visiting dignitary. And he knew the area well, with little stories about how easy the "birds" were to pick up at this spot, and how tough the bouncers were at that one.

"Now I tell you, lad, if you and me had the time I'd run us up to the old Columbia Hotel. Unless a fella' has your kind of size, or my kind of savvy, they've got no business going there at all. I'll wager a week doesn't pass but somebody gets shot or stabbed at The Columbia."

"And we'd go there because . . . ?"

"It's the girls, man, the bloody wonderful girls they've got; Prettier, friendlier, and cheaper than anywhere else in the whole bleedin' city. Good God, boy, the things I could tell you about those girls . . . "

And off he went, with stories about girls and fights and who knows what else. It was getting near one in the morning when we finally decided to stay put for awhile and do some serious drinking. Each of us started buying rounds and before long the table was nearly filled with our empty glasses. We didn't speak much then, content just to sit and get good and drunk while watching the other folks in the pub.

As conversations will when fueled with enough beer, ours turned serious finally, and personal. We'd both been recently divorced; me after six months of marriage, he after fifteen years. I couldn't really explain mine, and he didn't probe. The cause of his was simple enough.

"It was the beer," he held up his half empty glass and examined it a moment. "She could never quite understand that a man's got to have his beers and his time to relax down at the pub after work. That was really the only thing we ever argued about. I was determined to have my evenings at the pub, she was determined that I shouldn't. It took fifteen years to figure out that neither of us was going to change. Oh, sure, I might fiddle around with some friendly bird or other, but that wasn't the problem. I think it was just the beer."

The barkeep flicked the lights for closing time. We emptied our glasses and headed off up the street. He knew of a hole-in-the-wall eatery where you could get a whole plateful of Chop Suey for fifty cents, so we went and filled our bellies on the cheap greasy food. After, he took me across the street to a little bohemian coffee house and we drank cups of hot black espresso while watching a couple of chess players go through moves from the Fischer- Spassky game of the day before.

Our heads cleared a bit and he decided it was time to go home. We parted company on the sidewalk in front of the little coffeehouse, he going up the street to his forty dollar a month room and me to the freight yards. "Pleased to meet you, Yank," he called over his shoulder. I never did get his name.

IT WAS A lonely walk back to the freight yard. I was still pretty drunk and didn't at all look forward to the long cold ride I was about to take. Right then, all I really wanted was a nice warm bed to curl up in. But of course that was out of the question. I'd already stayed too long in Vancouver and didn't want to stay any longer. Like it or not I was bound to catch that 3 o'clock freight and be long gone by morning.

Walking improved my spirits a little, and by the time I reached my hiding place I was almost looking forward to the sunrise I'd be seeing from atop the Canadian Rockies. It was just then, when I was starting to feel good again, that I discovered my pack was missing.

All my possessions, my clothes, my gear, MY TRAVELERS CHECKS, everything I owned in the world was gone. In a flash I was everywhere, madly searching every inch of the freight yard, crawling on my knees, running up and down the tracks, climbing over old shipping crates on the loading dock; everywhere. I checked and checked again to make sure I had the right spot. I told myself that it must be there somewhere, that I couldn't have actually lost it. I cursed, I kicked the dirt, I cried, but to no avail. The thing I had depended on most during the trip, the very lifeline of anybody on the road, and it was gone; my goddamned backpack was gone.

"I'VE NEVER SEEN you here before," the young cop bent all his attention toward the suspicious looking stranger sitting before him. Clearly there was a working relationship between the night people and the patrolmen in Gastown. They all knew each other, by existence more than by name, I think. A new cop, a new hooker, a new anybody needed to find their place, and one way or another make their presence known. Nobody knew a thing about me, except maybe that I liked sitting on cold stone benches all night. I had mostly gone unnoticed until then, but now even Louise and the Indian quieted down, curious.

"I'm just traveling through, officer."

"Really? This doesn't look like traveling to me; it looks like loitering, and maybe public intoxication. Try again."

He was determined to have an answer he could believe, but I was reluctant to give it. The truth suddenly seemed like selling out; like confessing that, instead of being a mysterious watcher of the night I was just a dumb kid with nowhere to go.

"My pack was stolen. All my gear and most of my money were in a backpack that I stashed down by the tracks last night. I left it there to go have a few beers and when I went back it was gone. Figured I'd sit here tonight and listen for any word of it, somebody bragging about ripping it off or something. In the morning I plan on hitting the railroad office and the pawnshops to see if it's been turned in. I just came here because I didn't know what else to do. Is that all right?"

He considered for a minute, maybe judging the likelihood that I was lying, or pondering the stupidity of youth, or maybe just tired. Whatever his internal calculation, the conclusion he reached would save him some paperwork and me a night in jail.

"Sure kid, you can be here. But watch your step," he nodded at my bench mates. "Too bad about your gear. If you don't have any luck down here, come by the station in the morning and we'll see if we can help you out." He stepped back into the paddy wagon, then remembering why he'd stopped in the first place, he called back to Louise, "You stay out of trouble, grandma."

"Ah, fuck you," came the instant reply. He took no notice as the wagon moved on up the street.

Nobody said a word as we watched the paddy wagon round a distant corner and disappear. Darkness had now been replaced by a dull gray light as the sun grew closer to rising, and each of us on the bench sat wrapped in our own thoughts. Then, as if on cue, Louise and the Indian kid rose and started off toward Victory Square together. Without the sherry to fight over, the two of them didn't seem to mind each other, and they certainly wanted nothing to do with me. I had managed to slip into their world for a bit, but the simple truth had worn out my welcome.

Not long after a little French fellow came by and tried to proposition me, but once I told him my story he immediately lost interest. As the remaining darkness slipped away I had the bench all to myself. I have rarely felt so totally and miserably alone.

It was about seven that morning when I got around to asking at the railroad office and sure enough, there it was. A Canadian Pacific patrolman had seen my pack on his rounds and brought it in as evidence. Of course it was obvious that I'd been waiting for a freight, but because I hadn't been caught in the act there was no proof. With some reluctance on the desk officer's part, and after lots of quick answers on mine, I was finally reunited with my gear. Reeling from too little rest, too much drink and an overwhelming sense of relief, I crawled into the first empty boxcar I could find, not caring if it stayed still or rolled in any direction at all, and fell instantly, dreamlessly asleep.

SUMMERLAND
BRITISH COLUMBIA

August – 1972

THERE IS NOTHING quite like getting stuck when you're hitch hiking. I don't mean just waiting for a few hours for a lift, but getting really, honest to God, way out in the boonies stuck. Stop and think about it. What the hell can a guy do when nobody feels like stopping? Smiling doesn't seem to help, but looking sorrowful and lonely doesn't really get it done either. Lying down in the middle of the road might do the trick, but it might not . . .

That day when I left Penticton not a soul in the world wanted anything to do with me. I take that back. One old duck gave me a lift about fifteen miles up the valley, but that actually did more harm than good since it really put me out in the sticks. I wouldn't have felt so bad if no traffic was coming by, but that was just the thing, there were cars everywhere. The road was full of them, all out for a Sunday drive up the scenic Okanagan Valley, all having the time of their lives in the ninety degree August weather; tops down, windows rolled open and radios going like mad. Yes indeed, all of them having a hell of a time, and all of them, to the last merry carload, refusing even to acknowledge my existence.

It wasn't the individual drivers I was bummed about, after all, what did they owe me? I was just hacked at the whole bloody situation. I couldn't get a ride, I wasn't about to go back into Penticton, and the longer I stood in one place the more ticked off I got. The only thing left to do was walk.

If I'd been strolling there by choice, out amongst all those fruit laden orchards and panoramic views, I would have loved it. But under these circumstances it wasn't much more than a hot sweaty drag. Every mile or so I'd pass another solitary hitcher, or maybe some guy with his old lady. Just sitting there with extended thumbs and long faces, they'd look up as I approached and without a word tell me all about being stuck in the beautiful fruit basket of Canada; stuck, sweating, hungry and " . . . Aw shit man what a drag." Had circumstances been different we would have spoken, maybe even stopped to trade road stories. But on this hot August day all they saw in me was competition; someone who might ace them out of that hoped-for lift. Nobody spoke. They sat silently, and while they waited, I walked.

It was just north of Summerland, a small town where I bought some cheese and bread, that I came across the guy with the dope. Sitting cross-legged with his back up against a phone pole was this friendly little dude with an old Hohner mouth harp in his hand. There was a plastic honey jar shaped like Smokey the Bear on the ground in front of him. He smiled up at me from behind his wire-rimmed specs. "Howdee-do, why don't you sit for a spell", he said, and we were instant friends.

Damn it was nice to have somebody to shoot the breeze with; somebody who was in the same fix I was, and who cared more about being friendly than he did about getting a ride.

Down a steep dirt bank off the side of the road was a great big peach orchard; from the look of it the fruit couldn't have been more than a day or two away from picking. The kid said he'd spent the night before down there and that the deep green grass was softer than a son-of-a-gun. He had some honey I had some bread and the orchard had some peaches. It was quickly agreed that sliding back down that dirt bank to have ourselves a picnic and a sleep in the shade made a whole lot more sense than sitting in the sun by the road.

He was sure right about the grass under those trees. Soft, green and about two feet deep, it couldn't have been better. We sat down there eating our honey and bread with an occasional peach for variety. Those peaches were so thick and ripe that we could just reach up from where we sat to pick one of the dozens within our grasp, all as perfect as you please.

After we'd eaten our fill and talked a bit about the dubious merits of hitching in the Okanagan Valley, he reached into his big green canvas pack and brought out one of those one pound tins of Mixture 79 tobacco. He popped it open with the little key and there, sitting on top of the mostly full can and all rolled up in a plastic bag was his stash. Not very much, just enough for a few joints, but he didn't seem to care at all. He stared rolling, I got out the matches, and what a fine afternoon we did have.

Anything was all right with us. I took off my shirt, he kicked off his hiking boots and we both started eating like crazy. Peaches, peaches bread and honey sandwiches, and more peaches until we were both so full and so stoned we just lay back in that tall, fragrant forest of grass and crashed dead out.

It was the best sleep I had on the whole trip. I dreamed of fairy queens and magic kingdoms with enchanted gardens full of peaches; big, sweet, fuzzy peaches.

A couple of hours must have passed before we woke up. I can't tell you how tempting it was just to stay down there under the heavenly coolness of those trees. Just lie back down in that good soft grass and watch the days pass, with a belly full of peaches and a smile for everything in creation. The kid was already making plans for staying a second night, and I was seriously mulling it over.

By this time we had reached the point in our relationship where our decisions were made jointly, so he got out what little remained of his grass and asked if we should finish it up. I observed that we were both already about as mellow as could be, and after some careful consideration he agreed and put his stash back in the tobacco tin.

It was then that I got the funniest damn notion to go back up on the highway and try for a ride. To this day I don't really know why I wanted to leave that peachy paradise. It sure as hell wasn't because I was worried about getting any farther down the road; by that time I'd forgotten all about wanting to go anywhere. And it wasn't because I disliked the place; who could do anything but love a spot like that? No, I think it was because my slightly hazy mind told me I could just stand up there along that big old highway and simply charm the cars into pulling over. Yeah, that was it, I was going to smile the biggest, toothiest, most peach-eatingest grin you ever did see and just shame those people behind the wheel into giving me a lift.

The kid and I talked it over a bit and decided that, since I was feeling so righteous and all, we'd climb back up to the road and give it a whirl. He didn't want to leave the peach orchard though, unless he was sure of getting a lift. We agreed that he'd sit by his pole again, smiling and blowing his harp while I walked down the road a bit, just goofing along and smiling and not giving a damn for anybody. I was just gonna stick my old thumb out and smile away like a Looneytune until somebody stopped for me. And when they did, we'd swing by and pick him up too.

So we filled our pockets with peaches; me for the road and him for the pole, and off we went scrambling back up that crazy dirt bank to the highway. I say crazy because that's exactly what it had become since we'd slid down a few hours earlier and toked up. Every time we tried climbing the damn thing we'd somehow wind up back at the bottom, all in a sweaty tangle and laughing to beat hell. We must have screwed around on that hill for half an hour before finally managing to stagger over the top, still giggling so much that when the Mounties drove up in their shiny blue car all we could do was laugh at them. Somehow having a royal Canadian Mounted Police car drive up just then was the funniest damn thing in the world.

"Howdee-do." That kid had the most disarming way of saying hello that I ever heard. "Howdee-do there, how are you fellows this afternoon?" He'd told me he was from Alberta, but I swear it must have been southern Alberta the way he talked. "What can we do for you boys?"

"Do you have any identification?" It was the younger of the two Mounties who took the lead. From the look of his uniform and the way he spoke I'm sure he was the ranking officer, though the other cop was much older. The kid and I handed over our papers and stood there enjoying these two while they ran a radio check. Nobody said a thing as the minutes ticked past. My friend and I simply smiled at each other, waving occasionally at the curious motorists as they passed. We did our best not to laugh too much, and the Mounties tried manfully to look stern in the face of our good humor.

The radio let out a few garbled squeaks that, I suppose told the cops that we were not on the ten most wanted list; they both looked a little put out at what they heard. Then, just as we figured they were getting ready to hop back into their shiny blue Mountiemobile and blast off down the highway, the strangest thing happened. The older cop motioned for my pal to take his pack to the rear of the car, and the younger one told me to take mine to the front.

"Empty your pockets and place the contents here on the hood," the young cop was being very business-like, ready with pad and pencil to take down as evidence anything that looked even the slightest bit suspicious. "That's right, the front pockets too," he didn't know what he was letting himself in for. Already my wallet and kerchief were on the shiny blue hood, along with my 1971

Forty Niners football schedule and a gas station map of British Columbia. And he really wanted me to empty my front pockets and coat pockets too. "Pocket knife," he named each thing as I produced it. "Matches," he opened the cover and examined the half-dozen matches most carefully. "Assorted pocket change," both times he counted it there was only seventy-nine cents. "Coil of rope," he sniffed it. "Half pound of cheese," he tasted it. "Bic ballpoint pen," he looked inside the cap. And so it went, through all my pockets and my entire backpack down to the last pair of jockey shorts.

Things got a bit tense at one point when he found my pipe tobacco pouch. It's an old fashioned spring-loaded job where you squeeze the mouth and the tobacco comes out. When he unzipped it and saw a bent piece of spring-steel inside sticking up through the Cherry Blend he thought he had something. I got tobacco all over the ground and the car and my clothes trying to demonstrate how the damned thing worked. Finally I dumped the whole contents out in the dirt so he could see that the spring was just a spring and not a gun or a bomb or a miniature LSD factory.

Eventually there was nothing else for him to search. With my passport in one hand and a pencil in the other, he started asking questions, carefully calculated to make even the most hardened criminals slip up. I was glad to play along.

"Nineteen years old, aye?"

"Yes sir, that's right. Born September 26, 1952, just like it says in that passport, sir

"You a student on vacation, or just bumming around?"

"No sir, I'm neither. I am a Psychiatric Technician, just like it says in the passport. I'm fully licensed by the State of California and employed at the Sonoma State Hospital facility at Eldridge, California, at the salary rate of six hundred and fifty dollars per month. How much do you make, sir?"

He was not amused. "What kind of work does that involve?"

"It is actually pretty simple, sir. You see, we take crazy people and make them sane again. Nothing to it, really."

"Does your work ever bring you in contact with any hard drugs?

"Oh yes sir, definitely."

Now he was getting somewhere. All he had to do was get me to admit that I'd been popping pills at the hospital and he could throw me out of the country as an undesirable. There were a lot of us on the road in Canada that summer, clearly too many for his liking. I was obviously being cooperative, and a bit mouthy, so he was pretty sure he had me. For my part, I was just a little too stoned to care.

"Did you ever, at any time either during or prior to your employment take any of the drugs you were administering at the hospital?"

"Yes sir, I often took several of those drugs."

A hint of a smile crept across his lips. His older, more seasoned partner would probably have done a better job of hiding that.

As he took down every word I rattled off the names of half a dozen harmless drugs that most people have taken at one time or another. Things like tetracycline, ampicillin, monosodium glutamate, cascara and dulcolax. All of them antibiotics, food preservatives or laxatives and to the uneducated ear, each as sinister sounding as heroin or LSD.

Everything was going perfectly until I gave ascorbic acid as one of those deadly chemicals I'd been drowning. Somewhere in his past, probably in some men's magazine article about vitamin C being a wonder drug that will cure everything, he had seen the vitamin referred to as ascorbic acid. Now that knowledge bubbled to the surface.

"Ascorbic acid? That's vitamin C isn't it?"

"Yes sir, pure wholesome vitamin C, the best kind of acid there is."

And then he got it. He wouldn't even listen as I started back over the list explaining in detail the action and function of each drug I'd named. All that writing, searching and interrogation wasted on some smart-ass psychiatric something or other.

I could hardly wait to share what had happened with my buddy. His story would certainly be even funnier than mine. I was chuckling to myself as I knelt and repacked my gear, thinking about the good time we'd have scampering back down that crazy bank to our beloved peach trees; laughing, eating and maybe even smoking the last of his dope. We'd probably talk through the night, maybe even head down to the lake for a moonlight swim. And . . . oh, shit . . . dope . . .

Just as the realization hit me I heard the car door slam. I looked up over the hood of the Mountiemobile to see my little pal smiling back at me from behind the protective divider cage. They'd found his Mixture 79 and busted him on the spot.

What was great though, the very best part was that he couldn't have cared less. He just sat in the back of that big blue cop car, smiling that peach-eating grin of his and not giving a damn about anything. When they drove him off to jail he turned to wave at me out the back window.

I swear, he was still smiling.

TRANS-CANADA HIGHWAY

BRITISH COLUMBIA

August – 1972

THERE IS NO joy at three in the morning on these lonely miles of the Trans-Canada Highway, no joy and damn few cars to keep a guy interested. Not even any drunks to talk with or wine to share, as if I had anybody to share it with. Not even a thing in the world but those two lanes before me and the cold steel light-pole at my back. No excitement comes to save me here, no challenging road, no shining adventure. No girls to look at in this pitch black wilderness, no music to dream with, no world at all save the ominous shadowy tree giants that surround me and the flat gray highway at my feet.

I am tired to the point of exhaustion but can't sleep, won't sleep. Not here, not when a ride, or something else might come by. I'm not scared, but I'm not sleeping either. In the morning, in the light when I can get a look at things, then I'll sleep.

God how I wish I'd caught that train back in Vancouver. I'd be in Calgary by now, or maybe even farther. I'd be sleeping soundly as my boxcar rolled noisily on through the night and I'd be traveling still, traveling and happy.

The first day that Paul and I caught a freight, now that was really traveling; really sun-shiny, wind blow', busting ass by God traveling. Jesus yes, all the way from Eugene to Portland on the back of that flying, swaying, humping God-damned flat car, and not even caring. Not even having a care in the world as we rolled through those little Oregon towns; stripped to the waist, sweating like crazy, blackened from a week's crusted road dirt and not even caring at all.

And a few days later when we came down from Nampa on that mile long hot shot, what a ride. That gondola was just the thing for taking a long summer journey on a freight train. The car's sides came up a few feet so we could stand and look out as we road through the midday heat, a nice cooling breeze washing over us. Yet, lying down to sleep we were protected from the cold night wind but still able to see the sky.

Drinking strawberry wine and counting the stars we flew down along the Snake and the Columbia, waking at dawn to the sound of wheels and rails, looking out at the river and the trees and really being on the loose, really freedom flying. It didn't matter that we'd taken two days hitching to Boise only to turn around and head for Oregon again. It didn't matter at all just as long as we were out there doing it, out there feeling it, out there on the God- damned open handed face of the earth and living, traveling.

But the trip to Tacoma, that long lazy ride along Puget Sound in the late August afternoon, that was the best so far. The crusty old bad order boxcar with hobo chalk drawings, the waves and smiles from people as we passed, the long cool tunnels and high wooden trestles; smells of pine and salt water, diesel and life. The world from the back of a swaying freight on a mellow summer day; it was like a dream, a sooty, bumpy, noisy frantic dream. Sweeping us through the great northwest like two kings, that freight showed us the best nature had to offer. It rocked and lurched us through the countryside, parading the whole lush panorama from gently rolling ocean waves to snowy mountain peaks past our open boxcar door, and all for free.

That day I felt for the first time what every bum and hobo that ever lived has felt when they first caught that fast freight. They write songs of freedom and loneliness about it. They try to tell wives and families about it. They swear they've left it a hundred times but always go back. They run or climb or crawl onto a train to nowhere, just to feel their blood flow and their heart pound as they're slowly pulled and bumped and swayed back to that place where they once found peace, back to the road.

Back out on the road in front of me now it has started to rain a little. I can see a few small drops falling through the soft streetlight glow, and the highway looks speckled with the tiny wet spots they leave. No cars have come by since I started writing this, and I guess none are likely to now. My eyes won't stay open much longer, and it's probably safer sleeping off the highway than on it. I suppose the only logical thing to do is hike down into the bushes somewhere, wrap up in my sleeping bag and drop cloth and try not to get too wet.

If only I'd caught that train.

Big Al's

San Francisco

1973

Columbus and Broadway, almost 2 AM, and I'm starting to feel like a permanent fixture, leaning up in the doorway of the little Chinese hotel that separates Big Al's Naked Dance of Love from the seven nude, lewd and obscene shows at The Roaring 20's. I was supposed to get picked up here three hours ago, for the first shift of my new job driving all night delivery truck.

So far no show.

The barker at Big Al's hasn't been on his job very long either, so he isn't afraid to be friendly. Not like the veteran next door at The Roaring 20's, who keeps staring daggers at me. This kid is a real down-to-home type, from somewhere in Texas, he says. All he sees in me is a sympathetic ear after the fifteen-hour day he's just spent shouting at people who couldn't care.

Without once asking why I'm hanging around North Beach 'til all hours, he freely tells me the whole history behind his ending up as a barker in San Francisco. His telling is made all the more interesting by the fact that through it all he keeps shouting at passers-by so his boss inside can hear and won't come out to bust his chops or fire him.

"Ah, shit yeah, it ain't bad work for the money, that is if you don't mind yelling a lot."

"SEE THE NAKED, (he has a drawl, so yells "neeked") DANCE OF LUV, COMPLETELY LEWD, NUDE AND OBSCENE, RIGHT HERE AT BIG AL'S!

"Like today, I worked two shifts for twenty five bucks each, and I got ten percent of the tips, so that's a sixty buck day. And all I have to do is stand here and scream."

"YOU'VE READ ABOUT IT IN PLAYBOY, YOU'VE SEEN IT ON TV. NOW, COME IN AND SEE IT FOR YOURSELF, DIRECT FROM DENMARK, THE NEEKED DANCE OF LUV, AND THERE IS NO COVER CHARGE AT BIG AL'S!"

Truck Run

Stockton

October, 1975

I WENT TO Stockton today: driving flatbed and moving fast, pushing for time like always, watching the rear view and keeping my foot to the floor. Got to the feed mill quick enough, got the sixteen-footer loaded right away and started tying down for the return trip. I was jumping around the truck, tugging on ropes, cinching down knots, moving quickly, when I came swinging around the back of the rig and there stood this old man with a cane. An old wino I guess; eyes full of bloody veins, red splotches all over his cheeks. The guy smiled real friendly-like and came toward me like he wanted to talk.

I just nodded and kept on with my roping, not wanting to lose any time. He mumbled something and I swung on around the truck. While I tied off he came around and started mumbling again; sounding like he was saying words, but only mumbling with inflection. He smiled a toothless, drooling, lip-cracking smile and mumbled on, gesturing with his cane to emphasize the words he wasn't saying. I nodded and kept on working.

All tied down, I climbed up on top of the truck to check my load, leaving the old guy standing, mumbling to himself by the passenger door. The load was tight and I was running ahead of schedule. I swung down into the cab to make ready to leave. Out the passenger window I could see nothing so I figured the old fellow had taken off. I stashed my ropes, put the bill-of-lading in the glove box and turned to find him standing in my open doorway.

He mumbled some more. I told him I thought it was a nice day, too, and I reached out to pull the door closed. He moved slowly out of the way and I slammed the door shut. I kicked over the engine and released the emergency break. But the old wino was still there. I bid him goodbye and made as if to pullout, but he wouldn't move. His hand went into his pocket and he slowly produced a few pieces of change. He only had thirteen cents in the world he told me, this time without mumbling. His withered hand, holding his fortune, wavered in my open window.

He didn't ask for money because I didn't give him a chance.

"If all I had to worry about, Pops, was what to do with thirteen cents, I'd be a happy man," I said, bidding him farewell again and gunning the motor.

He looked perplexed as I pulled away. Then, seeing another trucker tying down close by, he forgot me entirely and headed over to try his luck again.

Down Bound Trains

California

Summer, 1979

The trip south was classic railroading.

It took half an hour to hitch a lift out of Fairfield. The fellow who picked me up was a carpenter headed to finish a job over in Lodi. The first thing we talked about was work, doing it and not doing it. He liked his so much that he'd been known to lay right down and sleep next to a job just to be close to it. Sleeping and working seemed to command about equal respect, his slight preference going to the sleeping side. His cousin, a geologist, was just back from Russia and Afghanistan. That got us to talking world politics until we stopped at a little roadside joint in Rio Vista for coffee. Then we headed out across the peat lands towards Lodi.

He'd grown up in that peat country. Sometimes there were fires that smoldered in it for years, he said, without being detected. They burned way down under the surface where they could not be seen, and without enough smoke to pinpoint the spot. Eventually some farmer would drive his tractor over it and down he'd go tractor and all, into the crater hollowed out by the fire.

We were about to the junction with Interstate 5 when he told me about his dream of getting a big house-boat and cruising the Delta channels and tracts, tying up wherever he pleased, living off the fish he caught and the produce he could work to pick or steal. He figured he could go for years without paying taxes, or anybody even knowing he was there. Like what I was doing on the road, he said, only he'd do it on the water. He let me off at the junction, and I'm pretty sure he spent the rest of his day, whether working or sleeping, thinking about that houseboat and those Delta waterways.

I was stuck for about an hour at the 1-5 on ramp, then a young fellow in an old '38 Ford pickup gave me a lift. He was on his way into Stockton to see about a new job as an apprentice tractor mechanic. Told me he had just signed off his current job as a detailer out at one of the boat yards on the Delta. A nice guy, the kind who introduces himself and offers his hand. We talked about farming and work, and about how working on the land has a special feel to it like nothing else. He didn't much care for his current job, and wanted to be dealing with farm people rather than the big money boys and blue shoes at the boat yard. He'd been born and raised right around there, and as we talked it became clear that he'd never left home and never really wanted to. Just a young guy who wanted to work on the land with people like himself. That was it: such small yet great plans.

About ten miles from the yards the Ford dropped me off. The ride I got from there was a real gem. A kitchen worker at the community hospital stopped and picked me up. Believe me you know this guy. Not personally of course, but you do know him; kind of crazy looking red hair, about forty pounds overweight, short and pudgy. You get the feeling that if you poked him a good one in the ribs he'd ooze. He was all decked out in hospital whites, and driving a beat up Opel Kadett station wagon that could do about forty miles per hour, tops. The minute I got into the car I had the guy pegged as a state employee. Sure enough, he had actually worked at Agnews and at Napa State, and was like a dozen guys I'd worked with at Sonoma.

He had all those weird behaviors that middle aged, male, state hospital workers have; it was really kind of fun just riding along and watching him go through his moves. We talked women, cars, women, money, booze, spies, and women. I knew the territory from long experience, so he and I had a fine old time. Though he was on his way to work, the guy took me, at forty miles per, all the way to the south end of the freight yard. As part of his accumulated wealth of strange knowledge he happened to know when the South-bounds rolled through, so he gave me a tip or two and set me on my way.

I was surprisingly glad to see that guys like him are still on the loose. They are a crazy bunch, seriously screwed up, but seeing one at close range again put me back in touch with something I'd missed without knowing it. Kind of the way a farmer must feel when he gets back from a long trip to the city and stands down-wind from the manure pile for the first time. The smell isn't all that pleasant, but at least it tells him he's home.

The Stockton freight yard is nothing special, just hot, flat and dusty like railroad yards mostly are. I sat tight for an hour in the shade of a beat up old flat car, then a few power units with a long string in tow came rolling through and I went for it. The freight was on the main line track so there was steep roadbed to climb up to reach the train. I hit the door of an open boxcar at about fifteen miles per hour, went to flip my pack up and in, and damned if it didn't flip like I remembered. That'll teach me not to load it so full next time out. In fact it came close to flipping back at me and knocking me off my feet. And by now the damn train was going like crazy.

It was a struggle, and a bit of an embarrassment, but I got my gear and myself into the car only to have the son of a gun stop while it was still in the yard. Actually it turned out to be a good thing. In the shuffle to get on

I lost my knit hat, so I hurried back up the track, found it there in the gravel and got back to my car just as she started to roll out. Not a very glamorous beginning for my return to the road, but if I was interested in glamour I wouldn't have been there in the first place.

It was, however, not the last time I was to be embarrassed before the trip was through.

The yard was in the poorest part of Stockton, in "The Barrio" my state worker friend had said. As the freight pulled slowly south I had a chance to take a good look around. It was a scene I had witnessed many times before, and was to see mile after mile on the run to San Diego. People don't pay much attention to what's in their back yards, particularly if they're poor, and poor people's back yards is where the trains mostly run.

The bad paint and busted appliances, sagging clothes lines and shattered windows that line the right-of-way run right through the heart of the country, are the heart of the country I guess. When you live with your backdoor fifty feet from a screaming freight train you don't think much about pretense or choices. You think of things like how to eat, how to have a good time, how to get through your life, and it doesn't matter a bit how much you earn or where you live. Cold beers on back steps; pretty girls in white summer dresses; old ladies playing cards under the trees are the things that line the railroad tracks. Watching those pictures unfold from the back of a swaying train is like seeing the actors after the play is over, just as people being real. For reasons I cannot explain I cherish that view of the country and hope never to lose the privilege of seeing it.

There is a string of small communities on the Southern Pacific line south, small old valley towns that I had never seen before, or seen so long ago that I'd forgotten them. My boxcar rolled through Ripon and Salida, Keyes and Turlock and Atwater, and it was a fine summer ride. When I caught the car only the west-facing door was open. At a stop down near Manteca somewhere I got out, hammered open the latch on the east-facing door and slid it back. The view then was even better; Highway 99 running down my left side, the crops of the great Central Valley down my right.

It was a pretty slow roll south on that first train; I guess it was a local but I didn't much care. There was heavy northbound traffic on the line that afternoon, and since we were a low priority train we spent a lot of time on sidings waiting for the highballers to pass. A few cars back from me there were three Mexican fellas going south for work. They didn't speak much English and I don't speak any Spanish. Every time the train stopped we would all lean out of our cars or jump down to stretch a bit; they'd nod at me, I'd nod at them. That was about it.

Seemed like everyplace we stopped there was a full irrigation ditch right in front of us. The fellows a few cars back would go over and dunk their heads and arms in, skip rocks, anything just to be close to that cool flowing water. I never realized before how present water is in that valley, arteries of it running everywhere through the earth. And the way the crops respond to it, with such lush growth and abundance, it's like all the wealth of the world is out there on those fields.

At one point I saw a farmer standing on his tractor seat looking out across acres and acres of fertile land, his land. I tried to imagine what that must feel like. To have such a bond with the earth, such a command over it must give those men an incredible sense of satisfaction and power. Then I thought of the bond my three Mexican friends had with the same earth. They too have a power over the land, but no more than it has over them. When the farmer looks out over his fields and thinks of what he owns, I suspect he includes the field workers as part of his possessions, like his tractors and his smudge pots. When the workers look at the land, when they hold its crumbling richness in their calloused hands, all they can call theirs is what sticks to their skin. It is the same land, and the people looking at it are of the same species, but how different must be the things they see.

After Merced the train started making better time. We didn't even stop in Chowchilla, just rolled past the little yard and the boarded up passenger station. Madera was the same; just a switch engine in the yard and a few cars, with some boys lounging at the herder's shack and the sleepy town all around.

It was dusk now. The setting sun had cooled the valley airs and the glare had left the sky. From my boxcar I watched the lights come on in the farmhouses, and the headlights sweeping by out on 99. It is remarkable how peaceful a freight train can be in the twilight; the sun sinking down, the car rocking back and forth, the cool breeze blowing in through the doors. I smoked a pipe, ate a little, but mostly just sat back and watched the show.

MY TRAIN BROKE up in Fresno. We pulled off the main line and the power left us on a siding at the north end of the yard. The fellows in the car down from me got out and asked me where the mission was in town. I told them I didn't know for sure, but gave them my best guess and they headed off in the direction I indicated. I don't think they even knew which town they were in.

There was a track shanty on the north end so I walked in for a drink of water and asked the switcher where the southbound trains were building. He didn't know much, but tried to be helpful. Between us we figured my best bet would be to stick by the main line tracks and keep my eyes open.

I headed south through the yards. Since there wasn't a tower to be seen I walked pretty freely and soon came upon a caboose at the end of a consist pointing my direction. It was right next to the main line tracks. I made my way to the head end, sat down on a flat car on a neighboring siding and waited for the power to show. In hardly any time three units rolled by, then came back and hooked on. I asked a yardman where she was headed. Bakersfield and Colton, he said. Once she was hooked on and the boys were nowhere to be seen I went for the third power unit, pulled the door shut behind me and laid low. Not half an hour later we were on our way. At least as far as Bakersfield I was assured of a first class ride in a soft engineer's seat, with a first class view to match.

I ate dinner in the engine, a can of tuna and a can of fruit cocktail. Somewhere around Selma I stretched out on the floor and got some sleep. The heat in those power units and the deep hum of the engines has always worked on me like a sleeping pill. Since I was by myself and didn't want to get pulled through Bakersfield or sidetracked somewhere, I got up frequently to look around. Mostly though, I slept.

A shift in the vibrations coming up through the floor finally woke me; the engineer in the lead unit had cut back on his power. I looked up to see the lights of the Bakersfield yard just ahead. It was still pleasant out so I sat in the open train window and stuck my face out into the breeze, drinking in the diesel smoke and the dust, and the warm night smell of the railroad earth.

We pulled through the long yard, then unhooked and shuttled back through a labyrinth of sidings and yard buildings, finally coming to a stop in the engine shops alongside a string of idling power units. I laid low until a yard guy came past and I motioned him over. Though a little surprised to see me, he was friendly and explained that my engine needed service and would be tied up for a few hours. I was awake and fresh and ready for more, so figured I'd try to catch something else. This was a big yard, well lit and with a big dominant tower in the middle. I shouldered my pack and headed for the darkest siding I could find. As luck would have it the darkest part of the yard was out near the main line. I put a string of cars between myself and the tower and headed south as quickly as I could.

At the south end of the yard, after about a mile's walk, I came upon a caboose with its taillight on; a good sign. As I walked slowly past I saw the light from the end of a cigar through the side window. I said Howdy. Somebody on the other end of the cigar said Howdy back. I couldn't see who was talking, but he sounded sociable enough so I pumped him for information. The train was going to LA he said, and the power had already been hooked on so she was about to roll. When I told him I was headed for San Diego he said that the

SP didn't run that far south. My best bet would be to transfer to the Santa Fe once I hit LA. He said the yards weren't too far apart so I wouldn't have any trouble. I thanked him and started quickly up the train hoping to find a good ride before she started to roll. I never did see his face.

The air was coming up in the train's brake lines; I could hear it squeak and squeal as I walked past so I knew there was no time to lose. The cars were mostly closed boxes with the occasional lumber car or tanker. Near the back were several auto carriers; noisy bumpy rides that I was hoping to avoid, particularly if I wanted to get some more sleep. About half way up the train I came to a bulk tanker that belonged to some chemical company. It would have been a pretty good porch ride in a pinch, but on the side of the car was a big warning about the contents, and an emergency phone number to call in case of leaks. I figured I could do better.

I was about two thirds of the way to the head-end when the train started to move. The closest thing that looked at all rideable was a bulkhead flatcar loaded with milled lumber. I'd heard enough stories about shifting freight and squashed hobo's that I didn't want to put myself between that lumber and anything else. Yet, without much choice except spending the night in the Bakersfield yard I figured I'd take my chances on top of the load, so up I went.

And out she rolled, gathering speed towards the mountains like somebody was chasing her. The view was terrific from up on top of the lumber, the warm desert wind in my face and the lights of the city receding as we headed south. As we drew closer to the mountains it started getting cooler fast. I buttoned up my jacket and got out my bottle of wine for a little warmth and comfort.

So long as I could stay awake I was going to be fine, but sleeping would be rough. Soon it would be too cold not to be in my sleeping bag. The problem was how to manage that without getting pitched off by the train. Awake I could brace myself, but I was pretty tired and knew I couldn't keep my eyes open all the way to LA. If it came to it I'd have to tie myself down.

We had just gotten into the foot hills, and from my perch up on the load I could see the lights of a string of power units waiting at a siding up ahead. I figured they were going to tie into our train for the push over the mountains, which meant we'd have to stop. I saw my chance.

We had hardly stopped rolling when I hit the dirt and started forward. There were a few dozen cars separating me from the head-end of the train, and the closer I got the faster I moved. I wanted a power-unit ride over the mountain if I could get it. The wine had made me a little sleepy, and my ride down from Fresno had me a bit spoiled. I knew the extra power would be hooked in any minute so I didn't have much time.

As I moved up the train I didn't see anything rideable but more lumber cars and knew I'd play hell trying to catch one of those on the roll. With no ladders to hang on to, no place to stand but on the load and half a bottle of sweet wine in me the idea of mounting a loaded flat on the move did not appeal. The closer I got to the lead units the faster I went, until with a dozen cars still to go I broke into a dead run, pack, uneven roadbed and all.

I hit the rear steps on the third unit just as the air was coming up in the lines again. It was warm, cozy and empty when I slipped inside the back door. I settled down on the floor, peeled off my pack and spent the next few minutes just catching my breath and listening to the train come to life around me. Then the engines dug in, and we slowly started our climb over the hump to LA.

I unrolled my bag and stretched out on the floor, but didn't sleep for very long at a time. One of my reasons for coming down the inland route was to see the Tehachapi Loop, the big circular grade that doubles back over itself as it gains height for the mountains. Every time I heard the engine shift or felt the train take an unusual turn I got up to see if it was the loop. Somehow in the dark I managed to miss it, but it will still be there the next time I go that way.

WHEN I WOKE up the next morning we were cruising through Palmdale.

Once over the summit it was an easy, slow ride down the mountains through Santa Clarita, Saugus and Newhall, and into the San Fernando Valley. As we came into Burbank and Glendale the train ran right along what had been the original highway through those towns, back before the freeway. It was the Barrio again, like Stockton and Modesto and the rest. Strings of old hotels had "Vacancy" signs permanently painted on their windows. Furniture dealers and hi-fi shops, liquor stores and taco stands lined our route. The buildings were old, like the highway that connected them. They had crazy paint jobs and funny signs out front. The streets and sidewalks were full of people; kids going to school, folks going to work. Some school kids were dodging in front of the lead power unit when we came up, but the hog-head didn't even blow his whistle. I guess he figured it wasn't worth it.

Across the street from a hair parlor two chubby beauticians were standing by the tracks and giggling. I think they'd put some coins down on the rails, and got a kick out of watching the train roll them flat. Some older kids chucked a few rocks at the train as we passed, and I was glad to be in the unit and out of their reach. The day before, up around Madera, a couple of rocks had come zinging through my boxcar doors, one bouncing just inches my head. Not everybody likes hobos, I guess.

We came to rest in the LA yards at 8:30 that morning. The yards are just about in old downtown LA, right where Figueroa crosses the LA River.

I packed up, hit the dirt and started for the south end, hoping to locate the Santa Fe yard. Some car-men I came across said it was about five miles down the river, and that an inter-tie train might be running that way sometime later in the morning. Sounded great to me. I went the mile or so down to the south herder tower, asked a guy there if he knew about the local, and he said it would be leaving for the Santa Fe yard in about an hour.

With a little time to spare I headed up town to get some breakfast. Had sausage and eggs in a nice little working man's café. The guy sitting next to me at the counter was a little crazy I think. He was about my age, drinking coffee and laughing to himself. Every time the counter waitress came by he held out a quarter to her and giggled. She would give him more coffee and he'd giggle more. While I was eating I guess he ran out of quarters. He looked over at me as if to ask for some spare change. The look he got in return changed his mind, so he went up to a guy who was waiting to pay his bill at the cash register and panhandled him. The fellow came across with some coins and in a second the spooky little guy was at the counter again, holding out a quarter and giggling.

From back in the kitchen I saw the manager kind of eyeing the guy, then he caught my gaze and raised a questioning eyebrow. I nodded. The manager came out and told the little fellow he'd have to drink his coffee somewhere else.

I picked up some groceries at a nearby market then went back to the yard to wait for my train. Only my train didn't show. After about an hour I started asking more questions. Turned out that the inter-tie wasn't going south for five hours or more; yard information works that way sometimes. A little disappointed, I figured what the hell it was only five miles. I'd been lucky with my rides so far, and was probably due for a little time walking the rails instead of riding them.

The tracks ran right along the western edge of the LA River. It isn't a river at all right there, just a huge concrete ditch a hundred yards across with a trickle of foul smelling water running down the middle. There were tracks on each side of the river, with spurs coming in from all directions. As I walked it became clear that this area had originally been the very heart of town. Every quarter mile or so a bridge crossed high over the tracks and the river. These were very old bridges, and beautiful, with ornate pillars and decorations; a glimpse of what LA had once been and would not be again.

It was hot along the river. The more I walked the more I wished I hadn't put quite so much stuff in my pack. A few miles along I came across some electricians repairing a signal box. Their gear identified them as working for Santa Fe, not Southern Pacific; a good sign. I asked where the yard was, thinking I'd be close by now. About five miles down the tracks, they said. I'd heard this five-mile story before.

Occasionally there were four-way rail junctions; places where another set of tracks crossed at ninety degrees to those I was walking on, and crossed a bridge over the river as well. Each had a tall tile roofed junction tower built in the Spanish style. Important places in their time, the towers were now run down and seemed mostly forgotten, made obsolete by electric safety controls that had long ago replaced the workers who once manned them.

At the Mission Junction tower a train was crossing in front of me. I sat in the tower's shade and rested while the freight rolled past. A scrawny old dog tied to the tower steps barked energetically the whole time the train rumbled by. I got the clear impression that he did that for every train. There was no sign of activity inside the tower or of who might have tied the dog there, but he didn't seem to care, lying down in the shade with is head on his paws as soon as the train was gone.

I kept walking; shifting my pack, stopping under bridges to rest in the shade, wondering just how far this five miles was going to be. At one point I saw a bum with some old rusty buckets scurrying down the steep concrete banks of the river. I don't know what he was after in the buckets. I hope it wasn't drinking water.

I'd been walking for a couple of hours when I came upon what started to look like a yard. There were strings of empty piggyback cars, but they appeared to have been sitting a long time. I walked along the cars, thankful that the walking surface was a little better. In yards the area between tracks is pretty smooth, but out on the line it is all rocks and my feet were starting to feel it. Turned out this was the beginning of an Amtrak yard and the piggybacks were just being stored there.

Before long I came upon several strings of shiny silver passenger cars. As I walked past I noticed that the doors were open on some of them and the tracks were rusty under their wheels. To get out of the sun I stepped inside one of the cars. I could see instantly that it had been completely trashed. Anything that could be broken was broken, seats and beds shredded, carpet torn up, fixtures ripped out of the walls.

I've seen vandalism before and it always seems stupid and pointless, but seeing those cars ruined was something else again. A train is a wonderful thing, a part of our history and our lives that is like no other. Trains brought us west, moved us and united us and helped us grow, and without them this country would be a very different place. But now we don't need them anymore, or we think we don't. The respect and awe and admiration we once held for trains is gone, and they've been reduced to rusty sidings and senseless rape. Like dinosaurs, they are big and strange and out of step with the times. If a T-Rex was to show up and walk the streets of LA I don't imagine it would get much more respect than those great old cars; fear yes, but not respect.

They had names like Pine Mountain, Pacific Cove, Indian Lake and Ocean Breeze. Seeing those cars so lost and sad made me understand that we will never witness their like again. The banks of the LA River seem like a strange place for a way of life to die.

DOWN IN THE heart of the Amtrak yard I found a track workers' bathroom with a sink and a john and an ice water dispenser. Like the trains, the place was old and beat up but at least everything worked. I washed myself and drank till I was almost sick; it felt so good not to be walking anymore that I didn't care. I must have stayed there half an hour, leaning up against the cool concrete walls of the place, taking trips to the fountain and resting my feet. I was sure I'd already come five miles and there wasn't a freight train in sight.

Another mile or so down the line I came to the Redando junction and figured I was getting close. A guy back up the line had mentioned the Redando junction when giving me directions so my spirits rose a bit. But a track worker resting up against the junction house told me I still had at least three miles to go.

On down the tracks I went and for the first time they turned and took a bridge across the river. Out in mid span, over the sick looking water, the smell nearly knocked me over. If the fellow I'd seen earlier with the buckets was drinking the stuff, he is surly a dead man by now.

Needing some food and a rest I made for a burger place a few blocks off the tracks, ate my fill and drank two big cokes. Somewhat renewed I started out again. Only, while I'd been sitting and eating my feet had been doing something altogether different. The blisters under my toes had filled up and my boots didn't seem to fit anymore.

After hobbling for several blocks it was clear that something had to change. I tugged off the boots and rubbed my feet through my socks for a few minutes. I didn't take the socks off because I didn't want to see how bad my feet actually looked. Luckily my running shoes were in the pack so I slipped them on, tied 'em real loose and started out again. If I hadn't had those shoes I'd be sitting there rubbing my feet still.

Finally, way off in the distance, I saw the tall light towers of a freight yard. By that time I'd walked out of

LA proper and was in a little place called Vernon, just north of Watts. Wearing better shoes and seeing those towers in the distance picked up my spirits considerably. I started walking quicker, feeling better, and thinking that I might one day get to San Diego after all.

Well before I reached the actual the yard I came to a piggyback loading station. It was a huge concrete affair with rows and rows of truck trailers lined up next to sidings containing strings of empty piggyback cars. Big walking cranes moved slowly up the rows of trailers, stopping over each one, reaching down with four long, spider-like arms and picking the trailers up to set them in place on the rail cars. I always knew it was done that way but had never watched before. The place was a bustle of activity, shuttle tractors running the trailers around at breakneck speed, strings of cars moving about, and the big crawling cranes inching their way along.

A handsome young Mexican shuttle driver pulled his tractor up next to me and got out. He asked where I was headed, and though his English wasn't too good he had an eager smile and warmth that said plenty. I told him what I was up to, asked him where the yard began and explained that I'd just walked down from the SP. He could see how beat I was, and kindly told me that the Santa Fe yard had begun, that this was part of it, and that the south end was under a distant overpass that I could see ahead in the smog.

I must have looked incredibly tired and relieved, because the he kept giving me encouragement, "It's only a little farther, you can make it, no sweat," he said. Then he reached in his cab, got out his lunch pail and offered me a sandwich. He hadn't been hungry at lunch and wanted me to have it. Having just eaten myself, and gotten the good news about the yard I wasn't thinking about food, or about form. I declined his offer, but thanked him repeatedly and went on. Thinking back, I wish I'd taken that sandwich, just to acknowledge his generosity.

A little more walking and there before me was the Santa Fe Yard. It had strings of bright red freight cars, a dozen or so dusty yellow engines near the herder's shed and a big central tower with lot of tracks. I don't know when I've been so glad to see a freight yard.

As it turned out I'd been walking on the main line so I just kept going all the way to the overpass at the far end. There was a track master's shack there, with a john and an ice water fountain. And just beyond it, in the shade of the overpass, a switch station with a few outdoor benches. The guys who made up the southbound trains worked from this station and I went straight for it. If anybody knew when a San Diego bound freight was leaving, it would be them.

An old track worker was at the station when I got there and he gladly gave me the lay of the land. There was a southbound going for Fullerton in a few hours;

it was now three o'clock. The San Diego coast express was due out at about 7:30. He warned me that there was a bull in the yard, but he hardly ever came down that way. Then he invited me to use the yard john, to drink all the ice water I wanted, and to wait on the yard benches there in the shade. I went for a long cool satisfying drink, got an apple out of my pack and sat down to watch the yard work and wait for my ride.

The next few hours were some of the best, most interesting railroad time I've ever spent. A half dozen switchers worked out of the little station where I sat, three engine crews, two engine foremen and a few car men. All types of men were there, friendly, quiet, curious, all types. We talked and swapped stories. Some told me about their work, about how good their jobs were; ten bucks an hour, six hours work for eight hours pay, no long trips, lots of benefits and no pressure. Others didn't show any interest in me at all, and a few clearly had the traveling envy I've seen so often. A couple of them, like proud little kids, strutted around the place, doing their best to show me that they were better at their job than anybody else.

I learned that it had been slow times in the yard for quite a while, that they usually finished their day's work in about five hours, and depending on who the yard master was on a given day they often got to leave early. One of the older guys expressed a little concern about the slowness, like maybe it had to do with more than the recession, like maybe it meant that rail freight was on the decline.

I didn't tell him about the Amtrak cars I'd seen.

It was a great, rich afternoon, full of good talk with good men. About five o'clock one of the guys came hustling out of the yard hut in a real hurry. He'd heard over the squawk box that some bastard of a car man had put in a call to the yard gumshoe, and that I didn't have a minute to lose before the bull would be there. 'Thank you" had hardly left my lips when I was sprinting across sidings and dodging around cars making for the yard limit and the safety of the street.

Once off Santa Fe property I made my way up to the overpass that ran above the switching station and crawled under the south end of it. From there I could see the yard and the station, but I wasn't on railroad property. I was even well concealed from the little service road that ran beneath me, between my spot under the bridge and the yard fence. There was a little crawl space; about three feet high right where the bridge joined the bank. I settled in there, enjoying the feel of the cool sand under me, the shade and the view of activity down in the yard. I had a few hours to wait but didn't mind at all since I knew when my train was pulling out, knew what track it would be on, and knew I would catch it.

I read a while, ate another apple and took it easy until about dusk. That's when I saw an LAPD car pull slowly along the road beneath where I was sitting. At first I didn't think anything of it, but then he turned around and parked right under me, right in front of the opening in the yard fence.

From where I sat, about twenty feet up the bank from his car, I was sure he couldn't see me without really trying. But I thought he might just try. I pushed my gear and myself as far back under the bridge as I could and laid down flat in the sand. I was back far enough that the crest of the little bank protected me from his view, but knowing that didn't make my heart beat any slower at all. For half an hour he sat and I lay there. I had the strangest sensation that everything had stopped, even out in the yard, and that everyone was waiting to see how our little game of cat and mouse would play out.

It was obvious that the yard bull was pissed at not nabbing me. Since he didn't have any authority off of Santa Fe property he'd called in some outside help. It was also just as obvious, to me at least, that I was going to catch that 7:30 coast express, bull or no bull.

Eventually the police car left and I breathed a little easier. Still, I just lay in my hiding place watching the yard and waiting. I figured the cop would be back, and that most likely I'd have him and the yard bull to contend with when my San Diego freight was ready to roll.

My best bet was to wait for darkness, then try to get myself into the yard just a few minutes before they sent the southbound power to hook on. That way I could beat the cops and still make my train.

I calculated the safest route through the yard, planning where I could use strings of cars and shacks to screen me from view, and when the time seemed right I made my move.

A fence separated me from the little service road, and another fence was between the road and the yard. When leaving the yard I'd walked right through the gate in the yard fence, and jumped over the road fence at the easiest place I could find. Now, though I still had to use the gate in the yard fence, I picked out a good dark spot to scale the road fence and went for it. Turned out someone had cut a hole through it right in the dark part where I was headed. I slid through, pulled my pack after me and ducked across the road low and fast. There was no sign of the cop.

Next it was through the yard gate, behind the switch shack, between a string of cars and I was safe. I leaned back to catch my breath, and as I did I saw the five power units moving out to make the hook-up, I'd timed it just right. Then I realized my coat was gone, it had been scraped off when I pulled my pack through the first fence.

Back I went, trying to stay low but going like crazy since I knew my power was about to hook on and the freight about to leave. I retraced my steps, took a few more risks to make time, got the coat and got back. The train was ready to roll and since I didn't have time to pick out a car I went for the last unit. I made the cab, sat on the floor and waited for things to develop.

If the yard bull had seen me, I'd know in a minute. If not, I was only three hours away from San Diego.

The train inched forward a bit, and just when I began to relax the door to my unit opened and a car man stuck his head in. "You ridin'?" he asked. "Yep," came my answer. "You work for the Santa Fe?" "Nope," I answered, "just riding." He closed the door and left.

I didn't like it.

As soon as he was gone I grabbed my gear and switched units. With the train ready to move I didn't want to try for a car farther back, but figured another unit might be safe. No sooner did I get settled in than the same guy stuck his head in again, and asked the same questions. I answered the same answers and he left. Maybe he thought I was somebody else.

This time I stored my gear and myself in the little bathroom in the engine's forward compartment, turned off the light and sat to wait. I figured it was too close to train time for the bull to get me, and I figured right. The engine revved up, I heard the air in the lines and off we went.

When we were out of the yard I sat up in the fireman's chair, opened the window and drank in the good night air. It felt great to be moving, not to be on my feet, and to have outsmarted the yard law. I was thirsty and tired but exhilarated, so I got out what was left of my wine and toasted the hot night, myself, and the fast San Diego train. All that walking, all that cat and mouse and all the blisters on my feet had been worth it.

I'd held her down.

We rolled out through Bellflower and Buena Park. When we came to Anaheim I could see Disneyland in the distance and wondered how many people had seen The Happiest Place on Earth from a freight, and how many had seen a freight from Disneyland. I thought about the people in Space Mountain and Pirates, and decided I liked my ride better.

There was a game in the Anaheim stadium and from my dark engine cab the lights were so bright over the ball field that I could hardly look at them.

We rolled through the old Anaheim station without even slowing down. Like a dozen stations I'd seen in those two days it was a beautiful old building, but all boarded-up, peeling of paint and plaster and bearing the scrawls and oaths of the kids in the area. Those places will be gone soon. Some will become restaurants, some museums, but really they'll be gone.

With my bottle of sweet wine I drank a toast to them as well.

I just finished my wine and was settling down to enjoy the coast run when we pulled to a stop at the Santa Ana Station. It was small and old like the Anaheim station, but Amtrak still used it for commute trains so it was still in operation. The train pulled through, stopped and unhooked a few cars, then backed them down into a siding.

As the units were backing through I saw somebody with a light climb up into the engine just behind mine. I should have gotten off the dark side of the train right then, run south on the tracks a ways and waited to jump back on as she pulled past me. But I didn't. Somehow the wine, the good warm night and knowing that San Diego was just a few hours away lulled me into inaction. I'd already done all the hard stuff, and didn't think I had any more to do.

I did take a precaution though. Figuring it was just a fireman or switchman inspecting the units, I stashed my gear and myself back in the little bathroom and sat in the dark waiting for the train to pullout again, but it didn't. I heard the unit door open then the door to my hiding place opened and there was a bull, with a badge and a light and a command to hit the grit.

I was busted in Santa Ana, on the San Diego Coast Express. And oh yea, the bull that busted me was a woman.

A bull, a yard cop, is a presence I have always held in my mind as being nasty, tough, scary and mean; able to put fear into the poor hobo with a mere glance. This bull wasn't like that at all. She was just kind of a hard looking middle aged woman, and she was actually pretty nice. It was impossible to feel abused by the long arm of the law when that arm wasn't hairy or tattooed or attached to anything but a pretty average lady just doing her job.

It may sound strange, but with this bull there was no romance in my bust.

She sat me down in her office, took all the vital statistics and looked my gear and me over pretty carefully. She asked if I had enough money to buy a ticket. So long as they took American Express I was fine, I said. Though I don't think she believed me, she walked me to the ticket seller, told him to get me a ticketed to San Diego and stood watching while I paid.

The Amtrak pulled in about forty-five minutes later. I boarded with the businessmen and kids and wives headed south, and sat down in a soft upholstered seat. I hated it. The car was clean and quite and air-conditioned. You could barely see outside because there was a thick window in the way, Conductors came by and stared at my gear and the way I was dressed. People in the other seats made casual conversation. It wasn't my idea of a train ride at all. I got out a book, pushed my reclining seat back and prepared to read the rest of the way to San Diego.

Somewhere near Oceanside I felt the Amtrak slow.

Looking through my thick black window I saw the Coast Express sitting on a siding as we passed. I'd left my empty wine bottle in the power unit. Suddenly I was quite lonely for it, and sincerely wished that I was back on that freight, keeping it company.

Catching Out

from The Last Professional

1984

Somewhere a hobo is waiting. He sits on an old wooden box, a small fire of twigs and branches burning between his outstretched legs. As he blows on cupped hands, the steam of his breath and the smoke of his fire rise to mingle with the other morning vapors.

His pants are gray and loose, his shoes brown and shapeless. The fire's near heat draws the scent of leather and earth and grass from his garments and these smells combine with the fire's own fragrance to make a rich and almost edible aroma. With quick breaths he drinks in the odors, his nostrils stinging from the sharp morning air.

All night he has waited by the fire, standing every few minutes to hold the lapels of his coat open and capture the rising heat. Hugging the coat closed tightly around him, he presses the trapped warmth into his skin, tingling until it is gone.

Now the sun is up. Its hot fingers are stretching across his shoulders, sinking through his jacket and through his back and into his bones. Now the waiting will be easier.

A sound breaks the morning silence, singular and unearthly as it echoes toward him. Again it comes, the sure, clear blowing of a southbound freight. His freight.

He knows every train that has ever run. Before he saw his first engine or heard his first whistle he knew. Gleaming rails have stretched through all of his life, through his dry lands and his mountains, through his cities, through his nights. He has followed them willingly, conquered them, owned them.

He has been their slave.

The hobo has no face, no age, no name. He has a need. Every moment that he's not on a train, he is waiting for a chance to catch one. Every moment that he's sitting still, he is waiting for a chance to go.

Slowly the engines rumble past him, jets of spark and black smoke pouring from their stacks. He kicks out his fire.

An open boxcar rolls up and the ritual begins. He breaks into a run, grabs the door, leaps. It's a maneuver that has cost men their arms, their legs, and their lives.

The hobo has done it since the beginning of time.

Over The Sierras

from The Last Professional

1984

The country outside Roseville is a gently tilting plain of grasslands and houses; tilting steadily upwards toward the Sierra Nevada to the east. It is a gradual climb that an automobile wouldn't notice, but the eastbound freight labored at it, all six of its power units throwing thick black smoke into the afternoon sky.

In their boxcar Lynden and The Duke rode like sailors on a rolling deck; hands clasped at their backs, feet wide apart, faces thrust forward into the wind. From standing all day in the sun their car was like an oven, so they pushed back both doors to admit a cooling breeze. At their sides the great brown landscape peeled by. Each open door contained the passing scenery like a movie screen, framing for them within those four rigid lines all the vast spreading images of the world.

Lynden looked out the door. Beside him the watery image of a shadow train was cast dimly on the ground. He remembered it. Silvery wheels were honed and polished on the anvil of the rails, and the air filled with their raw, steel scent. He knew the smell, and the smells of diesel and rust, and the roaring train sounds like the ocean in a shell. Through his feet he felt the strain of a hundred thousand tons, the hissing of the brake lines, and the wailing of the springs. Doors banged, metal slapped, dust flew. It was the train of his childhood, the train of his dreams; The Tramp's train. It pulled him like gravity, not downward but onward. It snatched him away.

Slowly the great train began to climb. Its route followed a ridge that rose gradually above the valley floor, and soon a wide, sweeping land stretched out to the south below. In the distance a row of palm trees crested a small hill, disappeared, then emerged again on the other side. Not far from the tracks a freeway ran, its billboards aimed hopefully at the heedless traffic speeding by. Horses grazed in dry pastures, and the unreal blue of swimming pools glittered like cold gems across the warm, brown plain.

The track began to twist as it climbed, and Lynden looked back to see the whole train come into view. "This damn thing's more than a mile long," he thought. He was right. It stretched back fifteen years.

In an hour they were in the mountains, climbing, twisting, driving ever deeper into the Sierra Nevada. Pine trees and huge Douglas fir crowded close into the tracks now, and the cars moved at barely a walking pace. The Duke no longer stood at the doors but Lynden remained.

In the evening's waning light he watched the rough-cut landscape take on a pastel softness: warm reds of earth where the track cut through a mountain side, muted greens and grays in the lengthening forest shadows. Night came, and still he watched. They were higher in the mountains now, and a harsh wind bit his face and eyes. He liked it, the sudden cold and dark. Outside, the clear night sky was filled with sallow moonlight. Great rock faces of the mountains rolled by, so close he could reach out and touch them.

Tunnels and snow sheds came more frequently, and drifts of snow were spread like white icing on the ground. The snow had a glowing quality, like cold fire he thought, and he imagined himself leaping into it. He imagined the thrilling rush of air as he jumped, and the gentle grasping coldness as he sank in.

A huge rock wall arose up ahead of the train. Fearsome and ghostly, it was the vast sheer face of Donner summit. Near its base a snow shed opened and Lynden watched as the train was slowly engulfed by it. One after another the cars were pulled in, almost sucked in, he thought. The mountain was inhaling, drawing freight cars along with its air. He watched the shed grow steadily closer, and watched the cold rock's gray-white veins spread like fingers towards the moonlight.

The other snow sheds had been short and filled with shadow. This one grew darker and still darker until there was no light or shadow left at all. Lynden clutched the edge of the door where he stood. He heard the magnified roar of the train, heard things swishing by the open doors, but he saw absolutely nothing. He touched the palm of his hand to his nose. He looked around in the car; at the noise from the other door, and to where The Duke was sitting. Nothing. He inched his head outside and looked toward the front of the train. A hot wind coursed roughly over his face. The smell was of diesel, and damp and mold. Bits of moisture fell on him, and his eyes began to water from the wind and blowing grit.

Still nothing.

Pulling his head inside, he closed his eyes and rubbed them hard. Then he could see, but no more than the familiar swimming colors of his own mind.

Lynden's sense of everything but the thunderous noise and the foul, stale air was completely lost. He floated in the blackness; a weightless body sailing through a shapeless void. He got dizzy and couldn't tell the train's direction until it lurched sharply and set him straight.

Unable to see or move he finally began to relax. Just as he'd watched the foothills in the daylight and the forests of the mountains at night, he settled back and watched the utter darkness.

When the train finally emerged it was like going from night to day. The sky above was now filled with a brilliant moon and stars that shown like a million small suns, their piercing light almost painful to the eye.

"They teach ya' about tunnels in those books?" The Duke had come up to stand with him. Lynden shook his head. "Tunnels 'been known to eat Gay Cats," the old man shouted above the noise. "Me an' some boys rode through the Moffit' with this 'Cat one summer, and damned if we didn't lose him. While we was inside the fool got up to take a leak, ya' see. Pissed himself right out the door."

Lynden felt the train's character change as it started down the eastern slope of the mountains. For hours it had been so slow and plodding, so pleasant and harmless as it wound and labored its way up the grade. Now it was gathering speed, lots of speed, and the harmless plodding beast was becoming a rolling threat. He could feel it through his feet, the tension and the power. A thousand brake shoes were applied, and the night air filled with the strange smell of their friction. The six power units now battled with all their strength, and the engineer with all his skill, to hold the racing train in check. Too quick a hand on the air, too rapid a reduction of the gears and the train could be wrenched from the tracks and smashed against the mountain.

The boxcar they were riding in began pitching wildly from side to side, its wheels screaming over the rails.

"You scared, kid?" The Duke shouted.

"Scared stiff!" Lynden yelled back. He was scared, but he loved it.

Alongside the Truckee River they ran, its rapid waters throwing darts of reflected moonlight into the night sky. The air got warmer, and soon a hot wind whistled through the boxcar doors. They were flying down the mountain now, rushing and swinging, hurtling toward the great flat desert below.

Whether it lasted minutes or hours Lynden wasn't sure, but finally the train began to slow. It rolled off the mountain and onto the flats, its frantic spell slowly broken.

They were in the foothills again and then out on the face of the desert itself.

And in the distance, like a magnet, the pulsing glare of Reno drew them steadily closer.

Susquehanna Thunder

from The Last Professional

1984

It was in Pittsburgh that Lynden saw his first railroad cemetery. A misty rain was falling, and his freight for Altoona had just eased out of the main yard. He was standing in the shelter of a boxcar and looking toward the river when the first dead rolling stock came into view.

There was a whole separate yard for it, every inch crammed full of derelict cars. Wabash, Milwaukee Road, and Penn Central they said; Soo Line, Grand Trunk, and Apalachee. A thousand of them at least sat rusting on the rails. The cars were scarred by accidents, slashed by derails, branded with the words "Bad Order" on their sides. Their paint faded, the once distinctive colors of two dozen proud freight lines now blended into a single muddy tone. Some were being lived in, others used as garbage dumps, but most just sat empty, wasted.

Beyond the forgotten cars were hundreds of power units marshalled in neat, desolate rows. Engines silenced, horns gone mute; switchers, main line diesels, even the awesome turbines had all fallen prey to the deathly place. "This is how dinosaurs die," Lynden thought.

As he looked out over them he felt ashamed.

His train rolled through Greensburg, Ebensburg, and a dozen small villages between. It was fast roadbed there, long new ribbon-rails having replaced the old. The train soon hit speeds that he'd never seen before. In Pittsburgh his mind had been filled with dark images, rusting trains, dying old men, but the racing freight changed all that. Its magic gripped him; its motions, sights, and sounds won him over as they had on his very first ride.

The crew changed at Altoona and he switched to a bulk car with a clear front porch. That put him outside. He could see everything now, feel everything, and forget everything that had ever come before.

Again the driving freight captured him. Dust clouds flew up along the tracks, wind roared louder than the train itself. Lynden laughed at the speed and cheered at the dizzy countryside flashing by. It was like that night in the Sierras; as if he and The Duke and the wheels and the rails were all flying through the mountains again.

Flying on one last incredible ride.

He stood now on the porch of his bulk car and watched the dark sky threatening rain. It was evening, but the thick clouds made it seem like night. His freight slowed some at Lewiston and he watched the town slip quietly by.

Then the lightning began.

At first a single bolt, then another, then many. Soon lightning ripped everywhere from the blackened sky. Its bolts cut jagged slashes through the darkness, burning themselves into Lynden's eyes. It started to rain, sheets and waves and torrents that pounded the landscape and set it swimming. Lynden stood far back on his porch, sheltered from the downpour but able to watch its fury. His freight raced headlong toward the heart of the storm.

At the banks of the Susquehanna River train and storm became one. Lightning struck so near that its crackling explosions dwarfed all other sounds, its flash sprayed the whole drenched world with blue-white fire. It struck out over the river, stabbing a bridge, a house, a town. It blasted right next to the train and Lynden felt punched by its hammering blow. The air smelled of power and rain and rails.

Thunder shook the earth. The furious night terrified Lynden, and thrilled him.

Then it freed him.

He was ready to go home.

End of the Line

from The Last Professional

1984

Winter sits heavily upon the shoulders of the mountain town. It is evening, the light is fading and a gentle, persistent snow dusts the landscape. From the windows of the houses warm lights shine, their glowing amber squares poking holes in the dimness and cold. Eaves hang with frozen cascades, chimneys are ringed with thick white smoke. The falling snow is all that moves, yet even it seems still. There is no whisper of wind; no sound.

Night comes and the white snow changes to blue. The green trees, the gray mountains and the swift brown river all shift their colors as well, deepening and blending into one rich indigo hue. The town is bathed in shadow, draped in gloom. Winter's thick blood flows sluggishly through its veins.

From far down the valley comes a familiar noise. A dog barks, a single dog with a single bark. There is silence for a moment, then the familiar noise returns. The mountains pick it up now, echoing it like a hundred noises before sending it on.

It comes again, louder, clearer. A beam of yellow light appears. It knifes and dances through the falling white night and gleams over the icy rails. Snowflakes run from the light, darkness surrenders to it. Then the thundering horn blasts and the northbound freight arrives.

Hissing and smashing, the giant steel beast groans to a reluctant stop. A kind of quiet returns. Power units hum and cars stretch, but the falling snow swallows their sounds. A banging is heard, a door banging on a boxcar somewhere back in the train. It bangs again, then slides open finally and a hobo steps into view. On his hands are wool stockings in place of gloves. On his head a wool cap pulled down low. He beats his body with his arms. He dances stiffly from leg to leg. His breath blows out in cold, misty clouds.

The man bends, jumps, and lands stinging on the frozen ground. He rubs his legs desperately, hopefully, and slowly the stinging leaves. Reaching inside the car he brings out a small satchel, then reaching again he brings out another.

A second man appears, a smaller man, and he eases down slowly onto the cold boxcar floor. The first man hooks an arm around him and lowers him to the ground.

They stand a minute, in the dark, in the snow; then the hobo lifts his friend in his arms and carries him toward the quiet town.

Eastbound Greyhound

Oregon

July 12, 1993

It has been a long time since I sat in a bus, in a station, in a seat that's too narrow in a town I'm about to leave. This bus is just over half full, and those of us who got on late were faced with the choice and the chore of deciding who to sit with.

One old woman climbing the bus steps just ahead of me took the first open seat and demanded to know of the kid next to her, "Is this one taken?" He thought for an instant of lying to her, and she saw the lie on his face. "You only paid for one, you know," she accused, and settled herself in next to him. With her bag and her cane and her sweater billowing around her like a sail, she took all of her seat and half of his.

I moved back slowly past the empty aisle seats, the windows going first, and decided how to decide; someone to talk to, someone pleasant? An older person to listen to and learn from? It finally came down to this; I'm taking this trip for myself, and it's by myself that I mostly want to be. I choose a seat, a third of the way back on the right side next to a short, quiet Mexican fellow who made no reply when I said "Hello".

I'm as by myself as I'm likely to get.

We're pulling out past the Union Station now, with its "Go By Train" command on the tower. Then across the Broadway Bridge and we're gone.

Only a few minutes out on the freeway and the Mexican man sitting next to me is asleep. I think he must be about my age. His hair is lightly shot through with gray, and his features, though smooth, have lost whatever innocence they may have once held. He has a thin mustache and stubble on his chin and lower cheeks. As he sleeps his hands are folded neatly in his lap. They are beautiful hands; the nails long and thick, the tendons taut even at rest. It is possible, even likely, that no one has ever looked at his hands in quite the way that I am looking at them now.

The bus is heading smoothly, steadily east, with logging trucks and foreign cars and a gravel rig called "The Midnight Angel" moving in the lanes around us.

Portland does not let go of us easily. The sprawl of it, from residential to industrial to rural somehow keeps hanging on, not really relinquishing its hold until the river is reached. I remember feeling this same grasp of civilization at the outset of previous trips along this route. But at last, with Washington on the left, Oregon on the right and the road and river stretching ahead, the vast inland expanse of the Pacific Northwest is spread out for our inspection.

We pull into a McDonald's parking lot in Gresham and take on two passengers: women in their twenties with "To Go" orders in white paper bags and a hundred extra pounds between them. This exit is all truck stops and fast food, and the turnoff to Troutdale Community College. I wonder if that school is as serene as its name implies?

And then, suddenly, we're in the Gorge. A double line of railroad track runs along our right side and the broad, shimmering Columbia is to our left. That last exit, it seems, was Portland's gaudy good bye.

What a sight the Columbia is. Right here, with Bridal Veil passing on the right and Multnomah Falls not far ahead, it's almost like Yosemite Valley has filled with water and I'm riding along its southern bank, expecting to see Half Dome around the next bend.

The river has gathered some clouds to it today; thick black-edged clouds that just scuff the tops of the ridges and peaks along the northern shore. If the sky were a face its expression would be somber, and just a little threatening. But ahead, to the east, lies a hint of a blue eyed smile.

We round a bend and instead of Half Dome see the immensity of the Bonneville Dam; mists rising from its spillways and power lines with voltage beyond reckoning rising from its turbines. For me this will always be Woody Guthrie's dam, and in many ways his river. "Roll on, Columbia, roll on."

Our bus passed "The Midnight Angel" at the side of the road a minute ago, he was checking his tarps. It made me smile to see him again.

Most everyone on the bus is riding in guarded silence, except the two Big Mac ladies who have talked non-stop since they boarded. My seat partner awoke for a moment, looked around then settled back down. I imagine that for him a few hours rest in a fairly comfortable seat is something to be valued, but maybe not. I don't know any more about his life than he knows about mine. To think differently is probably to insult us both.

We make a five minute stop in Hood River, for a stretch and a smoke and a nose full of the Greyhound diesel smell that is absolutely like no other. A handful of us stand in the parking lot by the bus shed, gazing out over the river and watching the barges and tow boats work against the current. There are dozens of wind surfers out there as well. From this distance they look like rainbow-colored dragonflies darting across the waves. We watch them out the windows as we get rolling once again.

Before the stop my seatmate awoke and spoke to me. He's going to Yakima, and guessed that I was going to Spokane. He said something else that I didn't understand. When I asked him to repeat it I didn't understand again, but pretended that I did. It's a start.

He is sitting up now, leaning forward on the seat ahead to watch the road and the country. He's wearing a dark blue windbreaker with white stripes at the cuffs and waist, and in his left jacket pocket, which is hanging half -open, I can see the foot and hand of a small cloth rag doll. It looks quite new. I wonder who it's for?

12:30 and we're stopped at The Dalles, dropping off a passenger or two. One is an old gent with an "NRA Patriot" cap and a not quite sincere smile. No, I'm wrong, he isn't getting off. He just stepped down to continue his one sided chat with the driver while the baggage is being transferred and the luggage tags checked.

A Union Pacific drag freight is pulling by on our left. Hoppers and grain cars mostly. No riders in evidence, and no caboose at the end. Soon all the cabooses will be gone.

I don't get any sense of The Dalles from what I can see here; it's just a place on a river and a rail line. It must be the most important spot on earth to a whole lot of people I will never know, but it's nothing much to me.

The Gorge changes here from green to brown, from rich to rigid; the cliffs and bluffs naked rock, the hillsides naked flinty soil. It is no less beautiful than the lower Gorge, but it could be a different river in a different country, even on a different planet.

Ahead of us a long freight train is crossing the river, stretched out from bank to bank; fifty cars in the dull colors of the road. It has two bright green Burlington Northern power units on the head end, and a BN caboose at the rear. I always did have a special feeling for The Burlington Northern.

Biggs Junction and time for a lunch stop. We must be back on our bus, #5467, by 1:30 or it will leave without us.

Got food from a little roadside deli; a diet Coke, a spring roll and a pizza pocket; all just fine as road food goes. I ate behind a gas station, in a vacant lot that afforded a view of the Columbia and the bridge north toward Yakima. A dozen sea gulls hovered around me most of the time, the wind so strong they could hold position a few feet off the ground and eye my meal as if it was their own.

My seatmate was standing at the edge of the parking lot when I returned, his bag in his hand. I walked up and we talked. He lives in Yakima with his wife and four kids, has lived and worked there for many years. He was just getting back from driving his wife's sister and her mother to Madera, down near Modesto. He is happy to be so close to home. His eyes scanned the approaching cars, looking for his family as we spoke.

And now I'm back on the bus, back on the road. I have two seats to myself, and I'm grateful for it. But I miss my mostly silent friend from Yakima.

John Day Dam is coming up. As much as The Dalles left me cold, the John Day feels real and solid and force-ful in the way that only a dam can; its might expressed not so much by what it produces as by what it withholds. A unit coal train, a Union Pacific triple-header, crosses the John Day River as we approach and for me the image of power is complete.

As the Gorge opens up ahead of us the sky becomes more open as well. Only a thin tracing of white cloud is now visible above the ridge tops to the north. The countryside, though still picturesque, is losing its drama here. The scale is too broad to be intimate, yet not broad enough to inspire awe. The river, the bluffs, the canyons that branch off and disappear into the hills --it is all of a piece somehow; stark, bleak, the same.

Then we climb for a moment, the horizon stretches out toward Idaho, and the blue Columbia seems to run right up into the sky.

A mother and daughter got on back at Biggs Junction and are sitting in the seats opposite from me. The daugh-ter must be three, the mother maybe thirty. She has the look of a woman taking a journey she doesn't want to, for a reason she'd rather forget. She asked the passenger behind her how long it would take to get to Pasco, so I don't think she has made this trip before. The little girl is quiet, happy. She saw me open a pack of Butter Rum Lifesavers a bit ago. Maybe before Pasco we can get to be friends.

I fell asleep for awhile, and now we're on the outskirts of Pasco. The country here is broad and featureless, and could just as easily be Kansas or Nevada or Saskatchewan. We got a glimpse of an intriguing suspension bridge just now, down near the center of town: all white and quite striking. Unfortunately it doesn't look like we'll get to cross it.

I just offered the little girl a Lifesaver.

She refused.

We are stopped at Pasco now and the seating ritual is unfolding again, only now I'm on the bus, not getting on as I was this morning. Several people got off, but several more are boarding. None of us who currently have two seats want to give them up. I've got my bag and jacket on the seat next to me. Others are taking the strategy of sitting in the aisle seat, making it hard for a newcomer to step across. One fellow looks like he's asleep; funny, he wasn't when we pulled into town. He is stretched across two seats and has been since we left Portland. I'd better clear the space next to me, just in case.

Looks like I made it: two seats all to myself. What is it that makes us feel just a little guilty if we get what we want?

3:45 and we're headed out of Pasco. Spokane at 6:30 if all goes well.

Stopped off for a minute in a little town called Connell. Mobile homes on Main Street.

The sky has grown larger somehow, its canopy of white and gray clouds spreading impossibly far in every direction. How could anyone ever have beheld this sight and not understood that the earth is round? Everywhere I look it sweeps and curves and rolls away from me in vast arcs and ellipses almost more felt than seen. There is a feminine quality to this richness and roundness, and Mother Earth becomes less a concept and more a real being as I watch her gentle expanse fold and undulate and flow to the horizon on every side.

We crest a knoll, and for an instant are truly on top of the world.

The woman sitting in front of me is Asian and not much more than four feet tall. Back in Pasco I held the door to the bus station open for her, and instead of walking around me she took the shortest route and went under my arm like a kid playing London Bridge. I must look like a giant to her. When I got back on the bus at Connell after stretching my legs I saw that she is reading a mysterious looking volume that appears to be written in Chinese. I want to ask her about it, but I'm afraid she'll tell me it's a romance novel or a textbook. I'm not sure I want to know that.

The road has turned into two lanes here, through what looks like wheat fields and prairie. There are no fences, just mile after mile of smooth, sculpted hills. God, this is a big country. And though every square inch of it is known to somebody, nobody could possibly know it all.

The folks on the bus are all pretty quiet now, reading or sleeping or watching the sky. An older man sitting one row up and across the aisle has his head resting against his open right hand, but the fingers are curled back against the side of his head and his thumb is curled under his ear lobe in what almost looks like a caress. The index finger is cut off at the second knuckle. The hand itself is brown and scarred and bigger than seems natural, I suppose on account of the work it's done. He may be about sixty, but his right hand looks much older.

Coming into Ritzville at 5:15. We make a fifteen-minute stop here, then the last push on to Spokane.

Back on four-lane now, straight and smooth through the grassland and the blue-white sky. The clouds are strangely low here, almost within reach; each insubstantial shred perfectly clear and distinct. And they are moving fast, driven by a wind out of the north and racing towards us as we race towards them. Their speed as they pass makes me almost giddy, their movements so reckless that I half expect to see them bumping and colliding with one another, or bumping us off the road.

A white haired woman sitting behind me just asked the name of the lake we're passing on our right. I looked on the map and told her I thought it was probably Sprague Lake. She agreed that it must be so. Her hair is quite long, and straight, and her clothes are right out of the late sixties. I think she'd like to talk to me, or maybe she really didn't know what the lake was called. Spokane will probably arrive before I find out which.

About thirty miles to go now and trees are starting to appear again. Not many, but after the long miles of absence these few seem an absolute profusion. Land can be pretty without trees, even beautiful, but to me it can never be entirely whole if trees are entirely missing.

By the time we reach Cheney the forest has actually returned, and I am glad.

I've been almost eight hours on this bus now: a few words spoken, a few new things seen. The first time I ever opened my eyes to this country was on a Greyhound bus much like this one, twenty-eight years ago yesterday. The ticket I carried with me all through that summer had a departure date of 7/11. My Grandma Olga, who saw me off at the station with my folks, told me the ticket was sure to bring good luck. I have never doubted that she was right.

It is beginning to drizzle out on the highway now, and twilight is settling over the landscape like somebody is slowly drawing the blinds. There is no red in this sunset, but the colors of pearl and sliver and old white linen are draping themselves across the sky.

And in the distance, in the fading light and the trees ahead, Spokane.

A Map of Oklahoma

June, 2001

I GOT TO Oklahoma City ahead of schedule. My business in Billings ended early so I caught a cab to the airport, thinking to spend a few hours in the lounge with a beer and a book, waiting for my scheduled flight. When I checked in the ticket agent asked if I wanted to take a chance on standby. Ten minutes later I was in a middle seat and in the air. The Denver connection went the same way: a few minutes on the ground, a middle seat, and airborne. I was supposed to arrive in Oklahoma City well after dark. When my plane landed it was only just late afternoon.

A rental car was reserved, but I almost decided not to take it. My appointment in Del City the next morning wasn't much of a cab ride from the airport, same with the hotel. But the car was reserved, and not taking it seemed like an insult to the person who'd made the arrangements.

It was a little sub-compact, four doors, twenty eight thousand miles on the odometer. I threw my carry-ons in the back, folded myself down into the seat, adjusted the mirrors and looked for the buttons to roll down the windows. No buttons. I cranked down the driver's side, reached across and did the same with the passenger, and turned the key. As the engine spun to life, a whisper of breeze glided across my face through the open windows. It got stronger as I pulled out of the garage and into the warm Oklahoma afternoon.

My hotel was only a few miles away, down a wide strip of restaurants, gas stations and discount stores. There was nothing remarkable about the street, but it felt good under my steering wheel.

I don't know that I've ever checked into and left a room so quickly. Two minutes, three at most: my bags were on the bed, my computer was on the desk and I was back in my rental cranking down the windows. I'd seen a convenience store on the way in. Got a bottle of water, some junk food to make up for the lunch I'd missed in Billings, and a map of Oklahoma.

I hadn't turned on the radio yet, and decided not to. I also decided not to look at the map. It wasn't to get me where I was going, because I didn't know where I was going. It was to get me home.

The first two-lane I saw was Route 152, and I took it heading west. Though the afternoon was drawing near to dinnertime, the sun was still well up in the sky. Traffic, by California standards, was almost nonexistent.

I wasn't thinking about Bruce. I wasn't thinking that exactly twenty five years ago he and Anne had gotten married in my back yard, and that next month he wouldn't be going on the backpacking trip we'd planned to King's Canyon, and that I'd never drink another bottle of his homemade beer. It had been three weeks, two days and five hours since he died, and I wasn't thinking about him at all.

Route 152 quickly found its way into the country. The tar-ribbed roadway clicked along smoothly, and the breeze through my windows picked up with my speed.

In only a few minutes I was rolling into a town called Mustang. My comfortable two lanes spread into four, and the countryside became a suburb. At a crossroads there was a sign for Yukon. I swung north on Hwy 4 and followed it, looking for two-lane again. Instead, just a few miles up the road, I found Route 66.

I headed towards El Reno, smiling to think of my little rental car humming its way west in the path of Tom Joad and Woody Guthrie, Jack Kerouac and Bob Dylan. "It's weird," I said aloud. "Really weird," I heard Bruce say, "but really cool." The passenger seat was still empty next to me, but Route 66 felt familiar beneath my wheels.

The sun was lower in the sky as I rolled into El Reno and too much in my eyes to keep heading that direction without the visor down. But I didn't want the visor, I wanted to see; as much as my windows and the late afternoon would allow. I turned right on Hwy 81, and Oklahoma opened up before me as the roadway cut north towards the Kansas border.

Now there was no traffic, and the side roads were only gravel. Concho rolled by, followed by Okarche; frontier towns more grown than built, and as changeless as the land around them. Clusters of oil derricks, like groves of leafless trees, appeared from time to time. Slowly rocking well-head pumps labored in quiet isolation, or sat frozen, waiting.

But it was the land and not the oil under it that drew me forward, and came up to meet me, and embraced me with the warmth of its wind, the smell if its soil, and the rolls and folds of its hills, streams and fields. It was the ranks of farm machines gliding in graceful unison through the early sunset light, and the dusty, lonely grain elevators, and the farmhouses old and beat and beautiful in their simplicity. It was the pickup with the dog in back, and the hotrod that flew by, and the tractor crawling slowly along the shoulder.

It was the land, and the wind that came from it and coursed through my open windows.

There were small signposts every few miles identifying Highway 81 as the Chisholm Trail, the cattle track from Texas where cowboys invented themselves a hundred and fifty years ago and took the road as their home. "Can't you just see them," I said, "the cowboys, and the Okies, and the wanderer poets from the fifties and sixties, all crossing this same ground."

"And all looking for pretty much the same thing," I heard Bruce say next to me. "I wonder why Oklahoma?"

"Maybe it was just on the way to someplace else," I said, but looking out at the sun as it touched the horizon I knew that didn't feel right. "Or maybe they really needed to be here, they just didn't need to stay."

"Maybe it was both," Bruce said, and we thought about that for awhile, and we watched the sun slide slowly into the prairie sea.

At Kingfisher there was a sign for Enid forty miles ahead and I knew at least that I'd go that far. The one friend I'd ever made from Oklahoma came from Enid, and though I hadn't seen him in twenty years and he no longer lived there, it didn't seem right to get that close and not see his hometown.

Twilight settled around me as the miles slipped by. The air began to smell like evening, but the wind still held its daytime warmth and flowed through my windows like a river. I flowed with it; through Dover and Hennessey and Bison, floating more than driving into the Oklahoma night.

Near Waukomis a local freight was setting out some cars on a siding and I pulled over to watch. In the dimming light against the purpling sky the freight cars were little more than shadows, almost more imagined than seen as they swayed and shuttled and nudged one another in the near darkness. But the switch engine, with its tracer light swinging and its engine droning and the resonance of its many tons vibrating through the ground, was very real and somehow reassuring.

It was mostly dark when I rolled into Enid and I set my car to wandering the streets. The movie theater and a few cafes were still open in town. In the neighborhoods nighttime sprinklers were watering front lawns, and front porch swings were more likely to be occupied than empty. I saw the lights of a ballpark and followed them to a slow-pitch softball game. The stands were scattered with families, kids were playing keep away just outside the foul lines, and the air smelled of barbecue and ice-chest beer.

The road east from Enid, across the Cherokee Strip, was wide and flat and empty. In my rear view mirror the last traces of burgundy twilight had vanished. In my headlights the highway beckoned.

"Let's see what this thing will do," I teased, knowing that I'd never push it very hard. I could see Bruce smile because he knew it, too.

But I did push it, surprising us both, and the wind came up to meet us as we picked up speed.

Now it was all about the wind somehow. Still warm and fragrant and full of the fields and farms it had crossed, it buffeted through the windows, roaring in our ears and drawing tears from our eyes. We didn't talk, because the wind would have carried our words away. We didn't think, or remember or regret. We surrendered to the sensation of the wind. For thirty miles, like dogs with our heads out the windows, we forgot everything and gave up everything, and became everything.

At the junction with Interstate 35 there was a sign for Oklahoma City. I eased off on the gas pedal and swung the car south.

There were truckers on the road now, big sets of doubles lit up like rolling carnivals and surging by just inches from my elbow. The highway wind began losing its warmth as the night deepened and the miles ticked by, but my windows stayed down and the wind stayed with me.

At Guthrie I took the off ramp and cruised slowly through the sleeping town, not because it was historical and not because of Woody, but because I was hungry. I can never recall actually craving Denny's sausage and eggs before. Now, nothing else would do.

Striking out in Guthrie I headed south again and in Edmund found what I was looking for. The parking lot was full of high school kids in ball caps, jacked-up pick-ups with their engines running, and the promise of a summer night. Inside it was the same; kids at tables in twos and threes and tens, kids working the counter and register, kids being kids.

Bruce knew and loved these kids, from a lifetime spent teaching in their classrooms. Being with them now, as I ate my food and watched them swirl around me, felt like an honor.

It was just after midnight when I found my way back to my hotel. The streets of Oklahoma City were mostly quiet, the air mostly still. I pulled into the parking lot, shut off the engine and cranked up the windows.

As I went to get out of the car I saw the map of Oklahoma. It had slipped down on the floor and lay there, unopened.

I hadn't needed it after all.

Following the Crest

West of the Pacific Crest Trail

July 21, 2003 - 7AM.

Ritch, Leigh and I left Salmon Lake at 9:30 yesterday morning. It was a good steady climb for the first hour or so; just right for getting used to our new packs and upgraded gear. This is Ritch's first time out with us. Last year Leigh and I spent much of our trail time planning how to lighten our loads. I was fifty-two pounds starting out last year, and dropped to forty-five this year. Leigh has shed at least as much. Ritch has heard us debating equipment weight all year on our trail runs, yet his starting weight is somewhere north of fifty-six pounds. It seems to be riding well so far, though I'm guessing that a lighter tent is in his future, and maybe some other changes. It isn't easy deciding what to give up, but harder still carrying things you don't need.

Our climb took us to a ridge top with clear views of Sierra Buttes and Castle Peak to the south, and Salmon and Gold Lakes to the east. We hiked the ridge for a couple of hours, then made a lunch stop at Oakland Pond. This was Ritch's first exposure to tortilla, peanut butter and fruit leather sandwiches. I'm not sure he's sold.

We picked up a jeep road and followed it west toward Snake Lake. During lunch we saw a few four-wheel drive rigs coming and going, and were concerned that a jeep run might be in progress. Turned out to be some guys trying to tow a friend up a ridiculously difficult stretch of road. Two days earlier the friend, fueled by too much beer and too much confidence in his Dodge Durango, had driven down this jeep track to Snake Lake and torn out his front differential in the process. His buddies were now winching him back up an incredible series of switchbacks and boulder-strewn washouts. We couldn't see how the Durango guy had ever gotten down there, drunk or sober. And we hadn't yet seen the worst of it. Several hundred yards farther along the jeep trail plunged down into the Snake Lake basin at an angle that seemed impossible to drive, and was nearly impossible to walk. We made it down; our experience telling us that no 4WD could ever make it up. Yet the very existence of the road indicated that some, at least, succeed.

We made camp on the west edge of the lake, on a high, flat clearing about a hundred yards from the water and only twenty yards from another jeep road. Thanks to an afternoon thundershower we got a chance to try our rain flys, and take an afternoon nap. I fell asleep instantly to the sound of the rain on the tent. Leigh stayed out by the lake and watched the light rain on the water. Ritch, who does not nap, was almost asleep in his tent when two more four-wheelers came by our camp. Ritch got up and went to watch with Leigh as the new fellows attempted to climb the impossible road up to Oakland Pond. And it did prove to be impossible; they turned around halfway up

We ate well, then spent a peaceful evening watching the twilight stars find their way through the high, broken overcast sky. The mosquitoes were present, but not terrible; the temperatures just cool enough to provide a welcome contrast to the heat of the day.

I rose early this morning as I tend to when backpacking. Sleep was good but not continuous; that's pretty standard on the trail. I was awake several times in the night, listening to the nocturnal sounds of the forest, watching the brilliant half moon come up like daybreak, just lying in my tent enjoying the unhurried calm that comes from being in the woods.

I made a cup of tea in the quiet pre-dawn, put on my mosquito net because they were out in clouds, then spent a marvelous, solitary hour out by the water. I don't know the names of the countless birds I saw and heard, or the names of the trees and bushes that were alive with their movement and song, and I don't care a bit that I don't.

Today we head a bit more west, to look for some Indian petroglyphs, and then on north to rejoin the PCT at the Four Hills Mine. This trip is the perfect combination for me, wilderness with a little history thrown in.

JULY 22, 2003 - 8AM. Lower Spencer Lake

We spent most of yesterday hiking on jeep trails, and though they took us to some great places we really came to appreciate how different they are, and how different the backcountry is when on a road. We will take trails anytime.

The Indian petroglyphs were either not there or we were looking right at them and could not see them. Yet we spent an enjoyable hour scrambling through brush and staring at cracks in rocks.

A hot jeep trail climb from the petroglyph site brought us up to Hawley Lake for our lunch stop. There is a Boy Scout camp there, thankfully empty, so we had the place to ourselves for a quiet lakeside meal. A Ranger and friend on motorcycles told us of more petroglyphs in the area, but we passed.

Another hour of climbing brought us to the Four Hills Mine. You never know what you'll find at an old Sierra mine site; sometimes just the barest traces of activity, sometimes actual buildings and equipment. Four Hills was an extensive operation honeycombing an entire mountainside. Large foundations, stone walls, rusted iron pipe and an old boiler were prominent. Slagheaps were everywhere.

At first it looked as though all the tunnels were closed. Then we spotted a slagheap somewhat removed from the others and saw that a small crawl hole was still open. Scrambling cautiously inside we found ourselves in a hard rock shaft blasted straight into the mountainside. Mining car rails were still in the floor, blasting boreholes visible in the walls. The shaft went back a good fifty yards before dead-ending. After the ninety-degree temperatures outside, the cool mid-fifties interior was heavenly. And it was a great thrill to discover this largely forgotten piece of history, and to actually get to explore it.

From our hillside vantage point we could look northwest down the valley to Upper Spencer Lake. We made our way down, on trails now instead of jeep roads. Upper Spencer is starkly beautiful; sheer cliffs on one side and no trees or shelter on the other. We pressed on to Lower Spencer, past a wonderful little waterfall that separates the lakes, and through lush garden-like thickets that were filled with more Sierra Lily than we have ever seen in one place.

From across the lake we had picked out what looked like an ideal campsite around on the southwest shore of Lower Spencer, and after some bushwhacking and false starts finally got here just before sunset yesterday evening. Surrounded by great views of cliffs, trees and the pristine lake, we made dinner to the sounds of twilight birds and the soothing rhythm of the nearby waterfall. There was a good breeze to keep the bugs away, and once the sun was fully down great stargazing in an absolutely clear Sierra sky.

July 23, 2003 - 6:30AM. Nelson Creek

We climbed out of the Spencer Lakes basin in midmorning, the views becoming more spectacular with every upward step. It was hot going on open hillsides for the first hour, then we plunged back into thick tree cover; glad for the shade and the wonderful forest smells. Soon we rejoined the Pacific Crest Trail and it gave us another hour of pleasant forest climb, looping out onto ridges and promontories just often enough to give us open views back to Sierra Buttes and the way we'd come. After being down in the lake bottoms those suddenly opening panoramas were almost heart stopping in their magnitude and beauty.

We paused for lunch at The "A" Tree. It is a junction of five roads and the PCT, and there's a good spring there as well. Much speculation ensued as to why this particular spot is called The "A" Tree, but to no avail.

While eating we were joined by a long distance hiker, the first of many we were to meet as the day went on. This fellow was doing the PCT in sections. Over the past few years he had completed Oregon and Washington. For this leg he is giving himself a month to cover six hundred miles, starting at Donner Summit and going north. He will average twenty miles per day. His pack, fully loaded, weighs just over twenty pounds. He explained that he had mailed himself food re-supply packets in care of General Delivery to strategic spots along the trail. His routine is to stop every two hours for a ten-minute rest. He has no tent, just a tarp, and no bear canister; he puts his food in a stuff sack and uses it as a pillow! But he does have tobacco and rolling papers; some luxuries you just don't leave behind.

We left him there at The "A" Tree, knowing that he'd pass us soon, and began the long, beautiful climb up to the ridge. Crossing over a saddle finally we were treated to marvelous views to the North and West, then we followed the PCT north as it dipped and swooped and meandered along the incomparable crest of the Sierras.

At a sharp switchback above a rocky prominence called Gibralter we dropped our packs for a long rest and look around. Two more through hikers passed us here; both had started in Mexico in late April, both were headed for Canada. They had so little gear and were moving so fast; it is nothing like our experience of the trail, and actually not very appealing.

We were also passed by a mountain biker with no gear and no water. He was moving fast to who knows where.

Ritch got stung by a bee, so Leigh and I scrambled up to a nearby snow patch and collected a bagful to put on the sting and reduce the swelling. Soon we were all taking turns putting the icy bag on the backs of our necks and wrists to chill our blood, marveling at how the coolness spread with every heartbeat.

A slow, hot descent followed, past volcanic pinnacles and close under the lava face of Gibralter itself. We were tempted to explorer its caves and lava pockets, but the long hike and heat were taking their toll. We elected instead to make an early camp if possible.

Our Pacific Crest Trail Guide described campsites on Nelson Creek, and we hoped to camp at the "fine" site it described well down the drainage. But when we got there it was taken. Though we were all mostly exhausted by this time, Leigh and Ritch in turn scouted off-trail to find a suitable creek side location for us.

I gratefully watched their gear, too tired to do much more than just sit.

When an acceptable spot was finally searched out we setup camp quickly. Then we made our way across hard, jagged rocks and out into the midst of Nelson Creek to wash our clothes and wash off the day's dust, dirt and sweat. Anyone passing by would have seen three bone-weary, naked guys splashing, gasping at the cold, and staggering over the slippery bottom on frozen feet

After dinner we celebrated Ritch's birthday with Peanut M&M's, then crawled into our tents and slid into our dreams.

July 24, 2003 - 6:30PM. Unnamed Lake West of Bunker Hill Ridge

We slept in after the previous day's hard hike to Nelson Creek. Down in that steep drainage the sun came to us late, and we enjoyed the long morning so much that we considered taking a layover day right there. But a careful look at our maps showed a small, unnamed lake up on Bunker Hill Ridge. It looked inviting; if there was water in it, if there were no jeep campers, and if the bugs weren't thick as smoke.

Several days into our hike now, our packs seemed to fit better when we strapped them on. We set out at our briskest pace yet, knowing we had a thousand feet to climb and at least seven miles of trail to cover. We naturally fell into a pattern of hiking that put some distance between us, so we were often out of site from one another. And we alternated the lead so that each of us could experience the wildlife, solitude and scenery enjoyed by a lone hiker.

Ritch came upon a pair of Western Tanagers close by the trail. I flushed a grouse from her trailside nest, and Leigh stood right in the midst of an eclipse of giant moths that looked like bumblebees. He captured wonderful pictures of them while they fed.

We hiked harder than on previous days, but took our packs off more frequently so the hot, hard climb passed quickly. On the backside of Mt. Etna we were close under spectacular volcanic formations, and the views got better and better the higher we climbed.

Our ascent culminated at Bunker Hill Ridge. Over 7,000 feet high, windswept and strewn with volcanic boulders and Mule's Ear, the ridge gave us spectacular views in every direction. We could see south to beyond Sierra Buttes, and to mountainous horizons at every other point of the compass. The lookout north of us, at Pilot Peek, seemed close enough to reach out and touch. A bee landed on Ritch's knee, hanging on tight in the wind as it drank from his perspiration, but not stinging. We scooped snow from a bank just over the north edge and used it to cool ourselves. We lingered, heedless of the time and utterly won over by our surroundings.

From the ridge our trail angled gently downward, and within half a mile we found the small lake we'd been seeking. There was a jeep road leading to the lake, but it looked little used. No one was there when we arrived, so we selected the best of the campsites available and spent the next couple of hours making a comfortable home for ourselves. We customized a log that we could sit or lay against, set up good clotheslines and rigged a water pumping station. Once the accumulated sticks and brush were cleared away and our tents were pitched we were ready for a good long stay. We will spend three nights here. It is a perfect setting and only a short hike out to the car on Saturday morning.

The rest of our evening passed with us watching the delightful variety of birds out over the lake. The Nighthawks were the most interesting; so fast and graceful, and with such elegant lines in flight. I turned in early after falling asleep against our log. Ritch and Leigh stayed up later, listening to an owl across the lake and looking for stars to peek through the cloud cover.

We had big winds in the night, and some rain. The flapping of our rain flys and pack covers kept us awake during the blow. And oh yes, during dinner last night Ritch and I heard what could only have been a bear growl, and it sounded close.

THIS MORNING I got up early, grabbed my camera and toilet kit and walked into the woods at the south end of the lake, seeking a suitable spot for my morning ritual. I got away from camp, over a ridge that was thickly wooded, and had just found a good place when I heard the snap of branch in a thicket thirty yards ahead. It sounded like a deer. I saw a flash of color that was reddish brown. There was more movement, then a leg, then a shoulder. Then a reddish brown bear's head with a black face. He was coming my way.

There was no thought of taking a picture. I hurried back to camp and stood with whistle in hand, ready to scare the bear, hopefully, and wake the others if he came. But he didn't. Though I heard him snorting and moving away through the brush he was no more to be seen.

Later in the morning I took my camera out again, and after sitting for a quiet hour caught a movement at the edge of my vision. Not a bear this time but a bobcat. It stood, watched, and listened as I got half a dozen quick photos. What an extraordinary animal seen in the wild, and an amazing bit of luck.

Shortly before lunch Ritch and I shouldered our stripped-down packs, marveling at how different twenty pounds felt than forty or fifty, and headed out in search of the Bunker Hill Mine. The map showed it a few miles east of us on the far side of Bunker Hill Ridge. We found it easily, though unlike the Four Hills Mine it took us a couple of hours of forensic archeology, scrambling up creek beds and through thickets, to piece together the particulars of the operation.

Leigh remained at camp, occupying himself all afternoon watching birds, resting, and enjoying the quiet.

We ate a pleasant dinner and watched the stars come up in a clear, cool sky as darkness fell. No owl, no bear, and our best night's sleep yet.

July 25, 2003 - 6PM. SOG (Slow Old Guy) Lake West of Bunker Hill Ridge

There were no unusual wildlife sightings today, though we did take a great hike down the western slope of Bunker Hill Ridge in search of the Slate Creek and Whisky Creek placer diggings. All three of us went this time, with light packs, plenty of water, and enough maps to make sure we got lost, which we did.

We did find placer diggings; we're not sure which ones. We had all seen the scarred hillsides of hydraulic mining from a distance before, it is hard to drive in the Sierras without seeing them, but this was our first exposure close up. Though it had been over a century since the huge water cannons blasted away the mountainsides exposing their very bones, we still felt as though we were walking through a skeletal and violated landscape.

Our intention was to go swimming in Delahunty Lake, if we could find it. Instead, we found Pilot Lake and a church retreat. The caretakers explained that it used to be called Delahunty Lake, then generously invited us to have a swim. I got video of Leigh going off an amazing rope swing contraption called The Flying Fox, and got a very red back for myself from doing a fifteen foot back-flop off the thing.

Clean for the first time in a week, and thoroughly refreshed, we easily climbed the thousand feet back up to our camp, agreeing as we walked that we three were well suited to each other, and to this experience. The day had turned out to be nothing like we planned yet it was exactly right.

July 26, 2003 – Back Home

It was an easy hike out this morning, past the Pilot Peak lookout station to Ritch's waiting jeep parked at the trailhead on the Quincy-La Porte Road. As we were stripping off our gear and getting ready to ride for the first time in a week, we met and chatted with a nice couple thru-hiking to Mexico. Young, fit and happy, we felt a bond with them that might not have been there a week earlier.

A family style breakfast at the old roadhouse restaurant in La Porte did a nice job of fulfilling our most pressing food fantasies from the trail. The Clampers Convention that we found ourselves in the midst of was an added bonus. Fat and either inebriated, hung-over or both, there were two dozen guys and gals in funny hats and rooster-red vests eating, shouting and generally making merry. There was every indication that they had been doing so all night long, in celebration of placing or repairing a historical marker just outside of town.

Silly as they seemed, it occurred to us that we had just hiked for a week with heavy loads on our backs, slept on the ground and eaten dehydrated meals that we wouldn't feed our pets back home. The Clampers mission, in addition to having a good time, had something to do with creating roadside monuments; ours had something to do with exploring and enjoying natural ones. Maybe that, and the funny hats, was all that separated us.

But it was enough.

CHIDAMOYO

ZIMBABWE

Saturday June 10, 2006

A SHORT DRIVE through the city gives us our first look at Zimbabwe and Africa. The current exchange rate here is 200,000 Zim dollars to one US, and officially inflation is at 1,000%. On the street it is actually 2,000% and going up almost by the minute. There are few cars on the roads as gas is unaffordable for all but the very richest. That leaves bicycles, hand-pulled carts, and walking, lots of walking. Buses are packed, but scarce. Traffic lights work, or don't; it doesn't seem to matter. And the advertisements are in English, the official language; so we pass endless upbeat slogans plastered on tired, beat buildings and crumbling walls, all seen from pot-holed streets

It is a five-hour drive to the hospital where we will be volunteering for the next couple of weeks. Ben, who has been here six months already, is behind the wheel,

Paul, a new intern just arrived from the Midwest is riding shotgun. Leigh and I are in the back. As we clear the outskirts of Harare it starts to actually feel like Africa.

There are hardly any white faces. A few tired old passenger vans are the only other motorized traffic, and they are filled to overflowing with those who can afford to pay for a ride. Two-wheeled "Scotch Carts" clog the road in some places, heavily laden with people and goods and mostly pulled by people. Cotton bales are stacked by the score on huge lorries, or balanced precariously, one at a time, on the two-wheeled carts. People carry amazingly large loads perched on their heads, and they walk everywhere.

The pavement ends not long after we pass through Karoi, and what little remains of the road is hardly more than a gravel track in some places. Ben is well practiced at navigating this route. He has guided the Land-Rover over it many times as part of his volunteer duties, and two weeks hence he will travel the route one last time as he, Leigh and I start our journey back home.

Small farms, called villages here, are visible by the road now. We see round mud-brick kitchen structures with thatched roofs and cooking fires that never go out. We see maize in drying cribs made of sticks and twigs. Cattle, sheep and goats free-graze everywhere and pay us no heed. But the people smile and wave as we blast past, even though we envelop them in a billow of dust.

We eventually reach Chidamoyo Township, a collection of squat mud-brick storefronts all selling the same meager merchandise. Not far beyond it we arrived at the hospital compound itself. In addition to the single-story, red brick main building Ben points out a church, a granary, a morgue. There are also living quarters of various description scattered around the grounds; some for staff, others for volunteers like us. Leigh and I get bunked down in a two-bedroom missionary cottage with a vine-covered veranda. It is plain, but much better than we expected.

Kathy, the Sister in charge, comes to check on us and invite us for lunch. We are in her company only a few minutes before understanding why this place survives in the face of such steep odds. Unassuming, friendly, dedicated and funny; she makes us feel welcome, makes us a wonderful meal, and makes friends immediately.

After lunch Kathy gives us our first look at the hospital. It is a remarkable place, providing far more comprehensive care than one might expect. They have a robust HIV/AIDS counseling and education program, a full maternity ward, a TB ward, a Pharmacy (though no pharmacist), and a lab (though no lab tech).

We meet the newly arrived Doctor Chinaka, a nice fellow just out of medical school. His inexperience is clear as we watch him and Kathy examining a new patient; Chinaka is tentative, Kathy confident. The twelve-year old boy's upper body and head are large and quite out of proportion with his lower body. He has a remarkable hernia-like protrusion below his navel, as if two fists full of intestines had broken through the abdomen at birth, and covered only by a thin layer of skin had developed outside the stomach's muscle wall rather than in. Neither of these abnormalities appears to be the immediate problem, however, which is labored breathing. No diagnosis is made.

The two days of solid travel finally catch up with us and we head back to our cottage for a long nap. I awake hours later, to a full moon and beautiful singing coming from up the hill. Drawn to the sound, I walk to the hospital's simple church and stand quietly in the warm, moonlit darkness, mesmerized.

As the singing washes over me and out into the night I feel as if I have finally arrived.

MONDAY 6/12/06

Woke up at 4AM this morning, read, and listened to the wind. There was drumming last night from a nearby village; a full moon is an invitation to be out and about since there is better light outdoors than in.

The fire stokers came by twice last night, stuffing logs into our outdoor water heater to guarantee that we would have hot showers this morning; very hot! Outside our front door just now roosters and guinea fowl are scratching in the yard as the sun comes up, and a young girl is passing by selling vegetables from a sack. There is a warm morning breeze.

Yesterday, our first morning here, we ate breakfast at Kathy's: strong black tea, scrambled eggs and ranch bacon. Then it was off to morning rounds and morning assignments. Leigh saw outpatients all day; more TB than he'd see in ten years back home. Paul helped deliver two babies, Ben did his normal routine; they will miss him so much when he leaves.

I was introduced to Oliver and Topson, the compound maintenance men. Kathy had heard that I was "handy" so as a result many projects were lined up and waiting; unclogging a water line, wiring an outdoor light, mounting a shower fixture, fixing an electrical plug. The most challenging of the day would be setting up an outdoor theater so Kathy can show World Cup soccer matches via her satellite TV and video projector. That one was touch and go for awhile; splicing coax cable without fittings is always an iffy proposition. But as Oliver said when we finished, "Today we are winning the race!"

Oliver is a wonderful work partner. He's about forty-five years old, was born in Chidamoyo Township and has been employed here for the past fifteen years.

He has five boys and a girl, and a small village nearby where he grows vegetables for sale. I enjoy his company greatly and look forward to working with him in the days to come.

We had tea at the hospital at 10:30; bread, peanut butter, and especially for us, fried mice. I passed on the mice but Leigh was game.

Oliver and I had a few more "wins" that afternoon, but there was one assignment we could not manage; repairing a non-functioning geiser (hot water heater). There are two in the guesthouse where Ben lives, but one has not worked for years so half the house has no hot water. We diagnosed the problem, a leak in the tank that cannot be repaired, so tomorrow we may attempt to run a bypass from the functioning geiser to the cold side of the residence. We have no galvanized pipe or couplings to work with, and I haven't yet located any pipe wrenches or thread-cutters. But we have been given permission to scavenge parts from an abandoned solar water heater elsewhere in the compound, so perhaps something will come together.

Leigh and I come to appreciate Kathy more and more. The pragmatism required when poverty is the norm seems natural to her, and honest, and not at all in conflict with her faith. She frequently sends patients home to die in peace rather than prolonging their pain here. And she will not recommend that a family with no money and no worldly experience travel to Harare in a last-ditch effort to save a dying child. She knows from bitter experience that the loss of their loved one would only be compounded by the huge debt incurred, and the abuse they would receive.

It is truly life and death here every day, but the consequences flow naturally from the circumstances and the grief, though quite real, lacks much of the drama one might expect. These people are sick, many of them very sick. They know that the hospital will do what it can for them. They are grateful for the effort, and accepting of the outcome.

Last night's World Cup trial run was a hit; the satellite video setup Oliver and I cobbled together worked! I had suggested to Kathy that she not publicize it, just in case, so staff were the only ones invited. But now that we know it functions properly the word has gone out. For 50,000 Zim folks can have great sideline seats at a World Cup soccer match, right here in the very middle of nowhere. 50,000 Zim is about a quarter US, and it is the same price the hospital charges outpatients for a visit and meds. Kathy has let it be known that she'd better not see patients at a game one night, only to have them turn up at the hospital the next morning unable to pay.

"Sister Katy" as Oliver calls her, is well respected in these parts, so I suspect her warning will mostly be heeded. Yet, with a World Cup game in the balance a few outpatients may select sport over medicine. And while Kathy talks a pretty tough game, I wouldn't be surprised if she sees them the next morning just the same.

TUESDAY 6/13/06

Leigh and I started the day with a four-mile run out through the country, past small farms and scores of folks walking to work and to school. The people we have met so far have been, without exception, friendly, gracious, and welcoming. Every smile we give is met with a wider one in return.

Today I went on morning rounds for the first time. We saw several TB patients, a variety of other conditions, and many expectant mothers and mothers with new babies; they do a hundred and fifty deliveries here per month. The protocol is that a family member comes and stays with every patient, sleeping on the floor next to the patient's bed; there to help with care, to listen and to advocate. And the patients don't stay in their rooms much. Their family members get them out into the air and light in the central courtyard as frequently as possible.

After rounds we observed a procedure on a young man in his twenties. His foreskin had remained retracted after sex, resulting in a condition that I can't name, and would not wish on anyone. The result is a combination of swelling and restriction that is difficult to imagine. The new doctor gave him a general anesthetic, then reduced the swelling by puncturing a series of holes in the swollen area, and finally making a slit in the foreskin so it could return to position. The procedure was not entirely successful because the condition was quite advanced, so the patient will be very uncomfortable for a week or so before returning for follow-up treatment.

Then we were off to an immunization clinic at a primary school about an hour's grueling ride away over the barely passable roads. Paul and I were braced in the back of a small pickup truck, and we got pummeled pretty much the whole way.

I've never had an experience like the clinic today. Close to two hundred moms and their children were receiving a variety of vitamins and shots. I took pictures until I had to stop, realizing finally that I would simply keep going until my camera quit, yet still not capture the simple beauty of the scene. Leigh was dispensing vitamin A to everyone, Ben was giving injections like a pro; I suspect he has given many thousands by now. I simply recorded it as best I could.

The weather has been marvelous, the countryside surprising. We are surrounded by gently rolling hills, lightly wooded in places and dotted with small subsistence farms, each featuring a variety of small outbuildings and a central structure, usually round and made of red brick with a conical thatched roof, where the cooking and sleeping are done. Most villages have an elevated corn crib outdoors where the maize crop is dried for use or sale. The staple food here is Sadza, a corn dish much like our polenta back home. Served at every meal with a different relish for flavor, Sadza is the fuel that keeps the country running. Cotton is also grown as a cash crop on many of the farms, and we frequently see women with bags of it balanced atop their heads as they take their small batches to the nearest purchasing point.

Leigh, Paul and Ben went back out to a second clinic this afternoon. I stayed behind to give my back a rest from the long morning jostle, and to setup the outdoor theater again for tonight's World Cup match. There will be no clinics or hospital work for us tomorrow. A government official is coming for an inspection and if "volunteers" are seen to be doing the jobs of the scandalously low paid staff then the government may discontinue their meager hospital subsidy.

WEDNESDAY 6/14/06

There was a beautiful African starscape as I walked back up from dinner tonight. It is not a familiar sky, and there are no constellations that I can easily recognize in this hemisphere, but the stars are brilliant and seem tantalizingly close with no competing lights to dim their luster.

I worked all day in the "Cold Room", a workshop that was just a mess of broken tools, castoff supplies and assorted junk when I dug in. I've whipped about a third of it into shape so far, and feel pretty whipped as a result. Tomorrow I'll see how much farther I can get.

We took a short hike to a mountaintop above the hospital before dinner. On the way I was shooting some video of an approaching scotch cart and the oxen pulling it nearly ran me down, not camera shy at all.

I'm nodding off between words as I write; didn't get enough sleep last night, and a hard day's work has wrung me out. Tomorrow perhaps I'll complete my organizing task. But now, hopefully, sleep.

THURSDAY 6/15

I put in a full day's work and completed my project cleaning and organizing the Cold Room today. Watching what happens next should be interesting. Out in front of the door there are now two big piles of miscellaneous junk waiting for final disposition. One pile is stuff that, to me, looks like pure garbage. The second and larger pile contains things that "might" have some value; broken tools, parts of oscillating fans, metal window frames and short lengths of pipe that have accumulated over the years. In the states I suspect that my entire junk pile and at least 80% of my "maybe" pile would get tossed. Here I know that a higher percentage will be retained, but how high? At least there is now clear shelf space to put it on.

Leigh, Ben and Paul did another clinic today, and came back pretty beat so we relaxed and watched the UK play Trinidad/Tobago on the big screen with a few dozen folks from the township.

Later tonight a Doctor from a sister hospital is arriving. Tomorrow he will begin training Dr. Chinaka to operate on Hydroceles; fluid filled sacks that surround a testicle and result in swelling of the scrotum. Back home they mostly occur in young boys and tend to disappear on their own. Here they can be quite large and are often seen in adult males. There are two or three scheduled for tomorrow, and I have been invited to observe.

The water pressure has been low all over the compound for the past couple of days, a problem with one of the boreholes apparently. We will be bathing with a pot of water poured over our heads again tomorrow morning. Not much of a hardship, really, when you come right down to it.

FRIDAY 6/16/06

My day began with observing and filming two hydrocele procedures in the Operating Room. What a rare opportunity to see this work up close, and to see and record Leigh and Ben, father and son, working together in this setting. My respect for the variety and quality of the medical work being done here increases every day.

In the afternoon I sat for an hour by the hospital entrance, just trying to capture the ebb and flow of daily life here. We are quite unusual as whites, and the camera is so out of the ordinary that it was hard not alter the scene simply by trying to photograph it, but I may have managed a time or two.

Mykwatch the O.R. nurse here honored us with an invitation to her village this evening. It consists of fifteen to twenty acres, planted in maize, sunflower, ground nuts, cow peas, and a local plant called "Bright Red" used for making jam. She and her children built the place entirely on their own.

She practices crop rotation, fertilizes, cultivates and harvests; hiring some of the work, doing much of it herself but overseeing it all. In a male dominated society she has defended her property rights, developed her holdings and consistently had better crop yields than most of her neighbors. Unlike many of the other villages we've seen, she actually clears the rocks from her fields and uses them for building fences and corrals. And she refuses to grow cotton because, as she says, "You cannot eat it."

SATURDAY 6/17/06

Leigh and I started the morning with an early run to a nearby reservoir; gliding silently through beautiful country along narrow paths through and past quiet villages in the still minutes before dawn.

After breakfast I spent the morning just sitting and filming around the hospital. I got one extended sequence of a family bringing their very ill husband or brother out into the courtyard. It was very touching, and personal, and right somehow.

Then I watched as Paul helped with a still birth. The baby was fully developed, but its skin was macerated, indicating that it had been dead in utero for some time. Incredibly, not five minutes after giving birth the mom stood up, got dressed and walked from the delivery room.

I did an electrical chore for Kathy after lunch, then read through her reference books on Zimbabwe. What a country this was, and could be again.

Before dinner I heard singing coming from the church up the hill; it was the youth choir practicing on the front porch. I listened to one song, then asked if I could film one and if they would sing me their favorite. They graciously obliged, and when I played the tape back for them they were delighted.

THURSDAY 6/22/06 8:45AM

I'm sitting in the courtyard of the hospital now, preparing to leave for Harare and home in an hour or so. Ben is on his last rounds with Leigh, Paul and Dr Chinaka. I think it may be awhile before Ben fully appreciates the impact this place has had on him, but he will.

There are a few patients and family members coming out into the courtyard just now, many more will appear as morning rounds are completed and tea time nears.

A herd of goats was grazing in front of me earlier but they have moved on. I hear the doctor's voice, and bursts of laughter coming from one of the wards. Young church volunteers, newly arrived from the 'States, are bustling about looking busy. Moms and their babies are lined up on the sunny side of the plaza. Uniformed staff are going about their appointed duties with quiet efficiency.

I am so impressed by how well it all works, in spite of the crushing poverty and collapsing country. When they need it most people get good quality care at Chidamoyo. Would more money, more supplies, better facilities help? Absolutely. But a modern western hospital would not be an improvement. Our rules and regulations, our fears and phobias would inhibit the level of patient care, not improve it.

Last night, in the company of several dozen folks from the hospital and surrounding villages, we gathered at our improvised outdoor theater to watch Ghana beat The Czech Republic two to zero in a World Cup semi-finals match. At the final buzzer the BBC announcer proclaimed, "All of Africa must be on its feet!"

I looked around me.

There in the very heart of Africa we were, in fact, all on our feet.

FORTY-FOUR
EMBASSY SUITES HOTEL, WASHINGTON DC

January 18, 2009 - 8:30 AM

FROM MY SEAT in the lobby I can see glass enclosed elevators gliding up and down, hotel guests on treadmills working out in the exercise facility, new arrivals rolling their bags along balcony walkways as they find their rooms. The clatter of the breakfast buffet is barely audible over the splashing of the indoor waterfalls scattered among the palms and banana plants filling the foyer of the Embassy Suites. Outside it is bitterly cold, in the teens; inside, warm and congenial, as much as a big hotel like this can be. If you have traveled at all you have seen this place, or one very much like it.

But I think it is safe to say that none of us have seen anything like what is happening in this town and in this country, certainly not in our lifetimes. Two million are gathering here, coming literally from every corner of the country and many corners of the globe. Many, like us, are coming to this event for the first time. Most are coming without any tickets, any connections or special "in" to the festivities and functions. Yet all are here for the same reason. They are filled with hope, and a desire to give form to that hope by being here at the beginning. They packed their bags and the warmest clothes they own and they left their cynicism behind.

We flew out of Sacramento, through Phoenix and Chicago. It was a reminder, once again, of how vast this country is. The snow capped peaks as we crossed into Nevada stood in stark contrast to the desert at their feet. And coming into Chicago in the late afternoon was like flying over a gigantic sheet of ice; no movement, almost no features visible to break the frozen crust of the world. Yet flying back out after dark, the millions of lights that burst from that frozen landscape glowed brighter than ever in the sub-zero cold, giving lie to the notion of desolation. There was life in that barren landscape, life and hope, brighter than ever.

In the shuttle from Dulles we were all Californians. Two fellows from LA, with pouches of newly minted Obama commemorative pins, had come east to change their fortunes. A family from Fresno; grandmother, mom, and adult daughters, were planning to meet other family members flying in from as far away as South Africa. A single woman from Oakland, who shared some chips with us during the ride, was going to stay with a friend. I have been in airport shuttles more times than I can remember. I have never been in one where the passengers so quickly became friends.

Yesterday we bundled up in every stitch of clothing we brought and walked the city. It was clear and cold, temperature in the low teens, and the town was beautiful. At the steps of the Lincoln Memorial we listened to Sheryl Crow do a sound check for today's concert. We just missed James Taylor doing the same, but heard him from afar as we walked past the Vietnam wall. How those performers will do it, in these temperatures, is hard to imagine. Our sense is that they would not be anywhere else.

The Capital Mall was fairly empty yesterday, the reflecting pond frozen solid. We walked and imagined what today and Tuesday will be like. Huge TV screens and speaker stands were already scattered from the Lincoln Memorial to the Washington Monument, those and more will clearly be needed. Some five hundred thousand people are expected to turn out today, there to listen to the music and to here Obama speak. We will be with them.

Everywhere we walked yesterday we found people willing to help if we looked lost, which we sometimes did, or eager to chat if we didn't. It isn't giddiness so much as it is openness. The usual barriers seem to have vanished; the usual defenses abandoned, at least for a time. There is this clear sense from the people we meet that friendliness feels good.

Yesterday afternoon we found ourselves at Union Station, and decided to see if we could get a glimpse of the Obamas as they got off their train from Philadelphia. There was no announcement that they'd make a public appearance, in fact there was every indication to the contrary. Yet on the off chance that we might catch a glimpse of the first family to be we decided to stick around, and we were not alone.

Imagine a football game where you've been told in advance that neither team will show up, but you go anyway. Further imagine that once you do arrive it becomes clearer and clearer that the teams really won't be there. Yet you stay in the bleachers just the same. You stay because the other people in the bleachers want to be there as much as you do, are enjoying being there without any expectation of ever seeing a kickoff, a touchdown, or even a player. We were all there simply because we hoped we might see the Obamas, and we chatted like old friends with all those around us.

Strangest and most wonderful of all, when it became clear that we really wouldn't be able to see them our hope was not replaced by disappointment. The hundreds of us gathered there had enjoyed our time together. We had enjoyed the expectation. We left somehow uplifted, not by Obama, but by one another.

I keep thinking of the lyrics to Stephen Stills' For What It's Worth. In the mid-sixties, when he sang "Something's happening here, what it is ain't exactly clear," we all knew what he meant because the ambiguity and uncertainty of our times was thick in the air around us. Now, over forty hears later, something is very definitely happening here.

What is happening is hope.

JANUARY 19, 2009 - 8:00 AM. Embassy Suites Hotel, Washington DC

There were more than half a million of us there yesterday; half a million. As we walked down toward the concert the sidewalks started to swell with the numbers as more people poured in from every side. Then we reached the perimeter, the streets were closed to vehicle traffic and the crowds spilled into them; a river over-topping its banks. There were National Guard detachments and Humvees at every intersection, there were cops on bikes and crossing guards dressed in fluorescent green from head to toe. And there were smiles, and greetings, and one monitor in her bright reflective vest waving her arms and chanting, "Welcome to my town . . . welcome to my town," as she ushered us along.

We came to The Mall at 17th Street and got in a security line with tens of thousands of others. T-shirt sellers took positions wherever they could, their wares displayed at their feet; dozens and dozens of designs all with a single theme---Obama. There were buttons for sale, hand warmers; posters, post cards and pins of every description. The Park Service was actually giving away commemorative buttons "To mark the historic event" a ranger said quietly when he handed us ours.

And the crazies were out with their hand-lettered signs, broadsides and bull-horns, warning of conspiracy, cataclysm, and eternal damnation for those who, among other things, watch televised sports---really. They mostly bemused the passing crowd, but when some started railing against homosexuals the throng would boo and drown them out. I don't much approve of booing, but gladly joined in. If there is such a thing as tolerant booing this was it. No one seemed to agree with these sidewalk preachers. Yet we all agreed that they had a right to be there and that we had a right to let them know how we felt about it.

As our line neared the security checkpoint to actually enter the concert grounds the checkpoint closed; that secure area of the mall had reached capacity. As people would leave others would be allowed in, but it was very clear that those in charge knew exactly how large a crowd could be managed safely. They also understood that no one should feel turned away, and we didn't. The huge TV screens and speaker stands we'd seen the day before were now alive with images and sound, so we simply moved to positions near them to watch the show.

The sheer scale of the event was breathtaking. From the steps of the Lincoln Memorial where the stage was located to the Washington Monument near where we were standing is almost exactly a mile. That entire span and more was full of people.

No matter how big the gathering you're really only with those directly around you. We stood with several thousand others in our general vicinity, close but not crowded, cold but mostly comfortable. We watched film clips on the big screen, we talked a bit, we looked around at the sea of people sweeping up to The Washington Monument behind us, and stretching unbroken to the stage which seemed so impossibly far away. We held up cameras to take pictures, we sent text messages to friends elsewhere on the mall.

We eyed the rows of portable toilets, apparently the most ever assembled in any one place; understanding that we were never going to make it there and back through the crowd and silently regretting that last cup of tea before leaving the hotel.

As the invocation was given by Gene Robinson, the first openly gay Episcopal minister, there was a technical problem with the speaker system; it seemed to be running at a fraction of its normal volume. Instead of getting noisier as most crowds would we got softer, quieter; so quiet in fact that we could hear perfectly. Half a million people standing quietly together, listening to a message of tolerance, hardship, understanding and hope, from a man who clearly understood the meaning of his words and who managed to make us understand them too.

The first music we heard was Aaron Copland's "Fanfare for the Common Man". It was banned at Eisenhower's inauguration because of the composer's politics. Yesterday morning, at the call of those trumpets I choked up. I didn't expect it and can't explain it, it just happened. And I stayed that way for the next two hours.

The program was a mixture of spoken word, historical film and live performance. An entertainment, a history lesson and an inspiration; joy leavened with learning, pure Obama. This guy means it when he says that we must expect more of ourselves. I think, from him it is a message, and a challenge that we are ready to receive. He spoke beautifully near the end of the concert, and the half million of us gathered there actually listened, closely, intently, almost hungrily. To say that we are ready for a change misses the point. We are ready for this change, in this time.

We listened to James Taylor and Sheryl Crow, Springsteen and Stevie Wonder, U2, Herbie Hancock and many more. Garth Brooks tore the place up with an improbable but incredible version of "Shout". Half a million people yelling "Shout" and raising their hands in the air is truly something to hear, see, and be a part of.

But it was old Pete Seeger leading us in "This Land Is Your Land" that I will remember most. Pete was blacklisted half a century ago for speaking his mind, and virtually banned from performing publicly. Yet somehow he discovered that no one seemed to care if he sang to children. So sing he did, in churches, schools and parks, anywhere he could find an audience. Slowly he taught a generation about folk music, what it meant, where it came from, why it was important. That was our generation he sang to, our generation he taught, our generation that helped make it possible to elect Barack Obama.

All these years later to see Pete on the steps of the Lincoln Memorial, welcoming our first black president, was just about perfect.

JANUARY 21, 2009 – 7:15 AM. Embassy Suites Hotel, Washington DC

We started walking well before dawn yesterday, a sliver of moon chiseled in the frozen DC skyline above us. We expected cold, wind, perhaps snow, so dressed as best we could for it. We also expected slow lines, long waits, maybe some impatience and frayed nerves, but we were ready for those. The concert with half a million people two days before had prepared us, or so we thought. But in truth no one knew what to expect. In its long storied history this town has never seen such a gathering, and may never see its like again.

The gates for those tens of thousands who had tickets would not officially open until 8 AM, the program was to start at 10. We were on the move at 6:30. Only official vehicles shared the cordoned-off streets with us, and even they had increasing difficulty navigating through the swelling throng as we neared the mall.

Our plan was to make for the rise just east of the Washington Monument, a full mile from the steps of the Capital where the swearing in would take place. This would be outside the official secure area where tickets were required, yet it would afford us the ability to get some sense of the crowd's size, and to see the ceremony via the giant video screens stationed there. We knew that to try to get closer would be folly, even at that early hour.

We were relieved when we reached the 17th Street entrance to find that there was no security check in place, and that the gentle slopes at the base of The Washington Monument were only just beginning to fill. We tried one location on the north-facing slope, high enough to see a good distance both east and west but also exposed to the bone-chilling wind. We soon abandoned it, settling finally on a spot in the more sheltered flats a few hundred yards due east of the spire. It would be our home for the next five hours.

Some brought lawn chairs, some blankets, some children were so tightly wrapped and bundled that movement was all but impossible and sleep the only option. We shared our points of origin with our neighbors, and spare hand warmers if we had them, and newspapers to provide at least a little insulation for those who chose to sit on the frigid ground. We watched the currents of people moving around us; the ebbs and flows as more and more streamed in and the empty spaces quickly began to fill.

Information messages flashed on the big screens; tips on how to stay warm, on how to locate a lost child, on what to do in case of an "incident". The silent prayer, shared by all of us gathered there, of all faiths or none, was that no such incident would happen on this day, or any day, to this man.

At 8AM the giant screens began to run video of the concert from two days before. We watched, and sang, and danced in place, stomping our frozen feet against the cold, clapping gloved hands, generating heat, passing time. Even though the sound and the picture slipped comically out of sync, when Garth Brooks told us to shout, we did. When Pete Seeger invited us to sing, we did. When Obama asked us to listen, we did.

When the official ceremony began on time at 10AM the giant screens showed the dignitaries taking their seats, the bands and choirs performing bravely in the cold, the motorcades making their way toward the capital through the strangely empty streets. And then an image came up on the screens, taken from a helicopter in the sky overhead. There we were, some two million of us. We filled not just the space from the Capital to the Washington Monument, but from the monument all the way up the steps of the Lincoln Memorial. A cheer erupted from the crowd, and a blizzard of waving American flags, clutched in the hands of hundreds of thousands, filled the morning air.

The hours that followed were packed with powerful symbols, powerful words, and the stirring images of a government and a people going through a unique and inspiring act of renewal. Yes, we do this every four years. Yes, this was the first inauguration most of us had attended. Yet we knew, all of us gathered there, that this time was different.

We knew because when the outgoing president was introduced the crowd's response was visceral, cathartic and completely involuntary. You might boo for a sports team you don't like, but this was a pure act of rejection; a collective body expelling an object that is foreign to its nature.

We knew because Obama's hand on Lincoln's bible, taking the oath as the forty-forth president of the United States, made whole a circle that has been incomplete since the signing of the Emancipation Proclamation. We stood with him at the podium, we felt the words as he spoke them, and we wept. Two million of us wept.

We knew because when the Reverend Joseph Lowery gave the benediction, the very timbre of his voice a testament to his lifetime of toil and struggle, he said what we all understand to be true. We must, after all these years of discord, " . . . turn to each other, and not on each other."

We must.

AVENAL JUNCTION

HWY 199 AND INTERSTATE 5

May – 2009

I SPENT SIX hours with "V" today. That is six more hours than I've spent with him in the last thirty-nine years, since we graduated from high school and he headed for Columbia University. His name wasn't "V" then. It still isn't anywhere but inside Avenal State Prison where no one goes by his given name.

He has been in Avenal over two years now, and he'll be there or somewhere else in the state system for another five to eight. It could be half that if the state is forced to reduce sentences because of overcrowding. Avenal was designed to hold two thousand three hundred and twenty prisoners, but now houses over seven thousand. That gives it two distinctions not shared by other California state prisons; it was the first to be built in a community that actually wanted it, and it now has the largest inmate population in the state, perhaps the entire country.

To visit "V" I first had to locate him, which required knowing his inmate number. I found that online, sent a fax to the California Department of Corrections asking his whereabouts, and in a few days received a reply with a mailing address at Avenal. Until that moment I did not know the place existed.

To actually visit Avenal I would need two things; approval from the CDC and approval from "V" himself. Simply showing up would not be allowed. You can't email an inmate, or call him or leave voice mail. He can call you collect if he has your number and you'll accept the charges, or if he has access to a contraband cell phone. I sent him a letter, explained that I was researching our old high school football team and that I'd like to see him.

When his reply arrived weeks later it contained a single handwritten page on coarse lined paper like you'd find in elementary school. Yes, he would welcome a visit, it said. It also contained a CDC Visiting Questionnaire that asked me several very pointed questions about my criminal history. On the back of the form it made it plain that in the event of an escape attempt, visitors taken hostage would not be recognized for bargaining purposes.

I arrived at the prison this morning at seven thirty. I wore the proper clothing; no blue shirts or pants as those are inmate colors. I had the proper money: no more than fifty dollars in one-dollar bills. I carried the proper identification: no wallet, just a driver's license. I brought the proper number of keys: one.

Though the doors would not open for visitor processing until eight, there was already a small crowd forming when I got there, mostly made up of women. Many of them were obviously acquainted from previous visits. Some had daughters, mothers, sisters or friends there with them for company and support. Most were alone.

They quickly recognized me as a first time visitor, and coached me on the rules. First timers often get something wrong and hold up the process for everyone. But even the old timers were surprised by the Swine Flu questionnaire we received at a quarter to eight. It consisted of four questions; are you sneezing, do you have a sore throat, have you been coughing, do you have a fever? Sick or not, everyone answered "No" to each. Most, like me, had driven many hours to get there: one family had come all the way across the country. No questionnaire was going to stop our visits now.

When the "Visiting List" was posted on the wall outside a few minutes later we all checked for our names, our inmate's names, and their current unit number. I was going to Unit Six.

The doors opened shortly after eight. We formed a line and filled out passes for ourselves listing our inmate's name and number and our personal belongings; one ring, one watch, one pair of eye glasses for me. At the metal detector we took off shoes, belts, jewelry, turned our pockets inside out, lifted our pants legs or skirts, and turned around once, twice or more until the guard was satisfied. We got our hands and our passes stamped.

The woman behind me whispered, "Lose that pass, and they will shut this place down."

To enter the compound we passed under a tall guard tower, and through a mantrap that penetrates the perimeter: two parallel fences topped with razor wire sandwiching a third, highly electrified fence between them. There was no sound of a cell door clanging shut, just the soft mechanical noise of the man-trap gate sliding closed behind us, then opening ahead of us to admit us to the prison.

Avenal, a dozen miles west of Interstate 5 and an empty hour north of Bakersfield, is surrounded by a remarkably broad, mostly desolate panorama of dry hills, irrigated cropland, and oil fields so old that the pipes and pumps and few remaining derricks blend seamlessly into the landscape. It is probably a perfect place for a prison. As we walked across the wide gravel yard toward vans that would drive us to our units, it was hard to reconcile the big sky openness of the place with the seven thousand men locked inside.

The Unit Six visitation room is like a small cafeteria. It has tables, chairs, vending machines and ceiling tiles in need of repair. The small round tables are the size you might find in a kindergarten classroom, the table tops scarcely two feet off the ground to prevent passing contraband unseen beneath them. Each table is numbered, and each has two chairs, side-by-side and facing the guard station at the front of the room. The officer in charge took our passes and our identification, not to be returned until we left. Trustees then ushered us to our pre-assigned tables. Signs on the walls reminded us that inmates were not allowed to handle either money or the vending machines. There were lists of other rules. No one seemed to read them. Everyone seemed to know them.

Slowly the inmates began to arrive, one at a time, and not on any obvious schedule. They wore light blue shirts, dark blue pants with "CDC Prisoner" printed on one leg, and blue and white canvas shoes. They were young and old, of every race and every size. Upon greeting their visitors they were allowed an embrace, even a kiss. Visiting mothers kissed their sons. Inmate fathers kissed their children and wives. They would be allowed one more embrace, one more kiss, just before parting. In between they could hold hands.

Each visit seemed to start with food; the visitor buying it with their stack of dollar bills, but the inmate making a point to prepare and serve it; heating it in one of the small microwaves, removing the wrappers, getting the napkins, waiting on their guest. Looking around the room I was struck by how absolutely normal it seemed, even in that abnormal setting: people sitting together, smiling, talking in low tones, breaking bread.

Some visitors had purchased photo tokens, called ducats, before entering. A trustee would take a digital photo, posed in front of an oversized painting of a streamside mountain cabin at sunset. There were no electrified razor-wire fences in the photos taken before that painting, no guard towers. Only families.

When my old teammate arrived we recognized one another immediately, and both confessed immediately that we'd been a little nervous about that. I asked how he'd ended up in Avenal, and he told me the story in detail, withholding nothing. Bad choices were involved and bad luck. As a result a young man died. There was also bad law. Appeals are making their way through the courts.

We spent the next six hours together, a couple of middle-aged men drinking sodas, talking softly about old acquaintances and old times, filling in the blanks.

Just two old friends visiting, though when I had to use the bathroom I didn't need to ask permission, or wait for it to be granted. He did.

For the over seven thousand inmates at Avenal time barely moves. There are limited jobs to go around, the library has few books and is rarely open, and programs for education or improvement are scarce or non-existent. There are the gangs to navigate. The contraband, the crowded dorms and the threat of casual violence are always present. There is the clock, the calendar, and the unrelenting open sky.

But on this day at least six hours passed quickly for my old friend "V" and me.

I'll be going back tomorrow to do it again.

Inca Road

Cusco

Monday 5/31/2010 - 10,912 Feet

THE GUIDEBOOKS SAY nothing about the Santa Ana District on the northwestern slopes of Cusco. From the Plaza De Armas you can see the city climb these heights, thinning as it nears the cluster of antennas at the valley's rim. I decided to climb as well, at least a little, to test my hiking legs and lungs in the thin air, and to seek an elevated view of the city.

The street climbed steadily at first, then angled sharply upward, the sidewalks along this cobblestone lane soon nothing but steep cement stairs. It was a cool morning, at least in the shade. I'd brought a bottle of water along, glad for the frequent excuses it gave me to stop and drink. To my surprise I was not instantly out of breath, nor was my heart trying to escape from my chest. The previous days of mild activity here in Cusco seemed to be helping, as was the coca tea and the Diamox. But taking this climb slowly, to enjoy it, was important on its own merits. As much as anything I think Cusco itself had been adjusting my expectations as well as my body's ability to function on less oxygen.

The grade increased, as did my pulse, until finally I reached a level spot with a commanding view of the city. Below me, a sea of red tile roofs; the churches now reduced in their dominance yet still the most prominent and identifiable features.

On the plateau where I rested was another large church, though it was far different from those below. Constructed of earthen bricks and closed for much needed repair, it seemed quite humble in spite of its size and prominence. I guessed this to be the church of Saint Ana, and as I surveyed the surroundings it was clear that the character of this crumbling edifice was in complete harmony with the district it served.

I continued past the church, seeking a better view of the city below and the neighborhood around me. To my left was a steep and rugged ravine, mostly screened from view by a crumbling mud brick wall. At a breach in the wall the ravine was revealed. There were homes, shacks, hovels; a few of cement block, most of mud bricks, some of castoff sticks and boards. They clung to the impossibly steep slopes in haphazard terraces and had no visible means of access. But as I looked closer paths became evident, some even paved. I took the first of these I intersected, and descended into a Cusco I had not seen before.

This was not like a refugee camp, where desperate shelters are virtually on top of one another and every inch is occupied. These were homes, humble to be sure but homes all the same. Though perched here and there wherever they could find a small level patch, they were at once both wildly unique yet at the same time clearly part of a community.

There were animals grazing and lying about, children in what passed for yards, men making mud and straw bricks from the materials at hand. There was corn laid out on tarps to dry in the sun. I was greeted with "Hola Amigo" by most everyone. The dogs ignored me. The children often smiled. The old men watched with quiet curiosity as I passed.

A narrow gauge railroad zigzagged up the west wall of the ravine, laboring first in forward then in reverse as it backed and forthed its way, switch by switch, to the top. I walked the roadbed for awhile, following its switch-backed course through the neighborhood. Where it cut through a steep embankment I found myself alone, and noticed some teenage boys above me, paying close attention to my passage. It was the only time I felt at all anxious, and probably without cause. But clearly, given who I was and where I was, had something happened the fault would have been much more mine than theirs.

6/2/2010 – WEDNESDAY – CHIQUISCA
First Camp – 5,115 Feet, 8:20 PM

I am sitting in our mess tent after dinner, with a cup of hot tea and a camp table to write on. The dinner dishes have been cleared away, and any doubts we might have had about eating well on this trip were dispatched as quickly as our meal. Trail food, no matter how basic, always tastes good. But what sets this cuisine apart: the savory soup, mountain rice and vegetables, the trout at lunch and chicken tonight, and the potatoes . . . the amazing potatoes . . . is that it really IS good.

We covered twelve miles today, much of it down switchbacks that tried to push our feet through the toes of our boots, all of it making our knees sing. Tomorrow we go up five thousand feet before lunch, a vertical mile that will surely produce other protests from other body parts.

After surviving the three-hour ride from Cusco early this morning, more a headlong flirtation with death than a drive, we stepped out of the car and into the pages of a National Geographic. For people like us places like this only exist in books, movies and dreams. All day we walked in a dream.

In the mess tent with me now, tastefully screened off in the cooking area by a fabric wall, are three of the team who are making this trek possible for us. Wilbur, the handsome young apprentice cook, just came out to ask how many liters of drinking water to boil for the hike tomorrow. It was Wilbur who set out soap and warm wash bowls for us as we came in off the trail today, and he has already asked what type of hot tea he should wake us with in the morning.

Effran is the senior man, a seasoned chef with many years of trekking and trail cooking behind him. He seldom shows his face, but our appreciation of his skills grows with every meal. He is talking now with Alex, our guide, as they both finish their suppers. Alex has told us that the cooks are curious to learn more about who we are, and he has set aside time tomorrow for them to get to know us better. From walking with Alex today we already feel we know him well. He is exactly the same age as our sons. As he guides and teaches us we cannot help but feel both grateful for his help and proud of his professionalism.

Domingo, our wrangler, is not in the tent chatting with the others. A small man with a ready smile and a spring in his step, every time he hurried past us on the trail today he hailed us with words of encouragement and picked his feet up higher, as if doing so would help us pick up ours. I suspect he is out tending his pack animals now, three mules and two horses; one of which they call the "Red Cross" horse. It alone wears a saddle, but it has no rider. Its sole function is to carry one of us out quickly should we become ill or injured.

Starting in Cachora this morning, the first hours of our trek took us past a patchwork of pastures and crops and small fertile farms along the valley floor. Where the trail began to grow steeper we stopped to rest at a handsome Spanish hacienda overlooking the settlements below. Its owners were gracious hosts, asking nothing of us and wishing us well when we'd departed. Only after leaving did we learn that, prior to the land reform, these people and their ancestors had once owned everything we could see.

As the hillsides steepened to cliffs it was surprising to encounter farms, though fewer now, that still managed to harvest an existence from the increasingly vertical landscape. What it must require to survive out here is completely beyond our experience, yet the Quechua people have been doing it for centuries.

The Womantay Range was to our north all day, a glacier-capped string of peaks soaring some twenty thousand feet above the Apurimac River. It is impossible to be this close to such mountains without being awed by them. It is impossible to walk the narrow trails, with a sheer drop of thousands of feet only inches away, without being humbled by our transience in this timeless place. On the steepest, most precipitous sections of the trail signs occasionally warned us "Do Not Lean". To lean out for a look would be to fall, and to fall would be to vanish.

At the high point of today's trek, a promontory that looked back up the river towards Cachora and down to Playa Rosalina, Alex asked our permission to make an offering to the mountains. We of course agreed, and he encouraged us to participate. Hiking off the trail to the very highest point, he turned over a large stone and took from his pocket a small offering of candy and coca leaves his mother had prepared the night before. Prior to placing them in this resting-place he blew through the coca leaves in the direction of each mountain we would encounter in the coming days. He asked each for its permission to pass. He asked them to protect us. He turned to us then, with a simple benediction to guide our steps through the rest of the trip. "Good thoughts, amigos," he invited, "Only good thoughts."

6/3/2010 – THURSDAY – BELOW CHOQUEQUIRAO
Second Camp – 11,055 Feet, 8:00 PM

Our first real glimpse of Choquequirao was across a deep canyon, a good ninety-minute hike from the ruins themselves. We had already climbed up more than five thousand feet from the Apurimac River, a steady and sometimes grueling hike of just over five hours. We went up the whole time, just up.

Until recently Choquequirao lay hidden from view, obscured by the jungle for over five hundred years. Today it began to reveal its secrets to us slowly as we approached, in much the same way that it has gradually revealed itself to the world as the jungle has been painstakingly beaten back.

At first we saw a suggestion of the main plaza structures above us and across the canyon. The distance made any appreciation of scale impossible. Our trail rounded a turn, opening up a view of the steep slopes far below the ruin. We saw perched there, at the very edge of a thousand-foot precipice, a cluster of terraces emerging from the jungle. A look with binoculars showed us that these were no small constructions, but broad flat terraced steps perhaps twenty feet across, perhaps forty, marching for hundreds of feet up the amazingly steep slope.

There is no guidebook for Choquequirao, there are no maps. There are only trekkers like us, who, with the help of our guides are discovering the place for the first time. We spoke in awe of the engineering required. We were amazed at the scope and scale of the terrace network. Then the trail took another bend, opening up another view, and we beheld a new terrace network at least ten times bigger than the first. The effect was almost intoxicating.

We had worked very hard to get there, and couldn't wait to actually set foot in the complex, but the Andes will have their due. It took another hour to actually reach the site, much of it very steep, all of it up. It was only fatigue, and the limitations of my body that prevented me from running the whole way.

We had just over two hours to explore the ruin complex itself. Any longer and we'd lose the light, and risk coming down the treacherous trail to our campsite with nothing but our headlamps to guide us. In many ways two hours was not nearly enough, yet it is impossible to complain about having any time at all in such an extraordinary place. We explored with enthusiasm and wonder, glad for every minute.

It is clear that the Inca architects valued nature, and at Choquequirao they capitalized on it to amazing effect. The complex sits in a saddle, a high round ceremonial plateau anchoring the south end, a cluster of springs and stone houses climbing the steep slope to the north. From this northern rampart you look straight down to the Apurimac, a mile below. Another trekker joined us at the edge, looked down, and without a hint of exaggeration said, "This is the best view in the world".

Tomorrow we will be up at 5 AM and on the trail by 6. For the first hour and a half we will be hiking almost straight up, our trail taking us over the steep mountain ridge that serves as Choquequirao's northern backdrop. Those final views overlooking the complex will likely be our last.

6/4/2010 – Friday – Maizal
Third Camp – 9,900 Feet, 8:30 PM

We knew last night that today would be our hardest, Alex warned us in advance. Starting out at 6:15 we climbed more than a thousand feet through the Andean cloud forest; a mountaintop jungle fed by tropical rains in the wet season, and literally watered by a blanket of dense, enfolding clouds the rest of the year. On our way up we passed a section of the original Inca aqueduct that supplied water to Choquequirao hundreds of feet below and more than a mile away; a stone umbilical from the very heavens themselves.

We rounded a promontory at eleven thousand feet, the trail often slick with mud, the drop many thousands of feet should we make a misstep, and got a pulse-stopping look at our mid-day destination, the Rio Blanco more than a mile below. On this leg of our journey we have left the commonly used trails behind, and for three days will be following narrow footpaths used almost exclusively by the Quechua people who inhabit these remote mountains. Most trekkers in these parts take either the five day Choquequirao loop, the first half of which we have just completed, or the five day Salkantay trek, the last portion of which we will be picking up three days hence. Our course now connects these two, a tenuous linkage that makes the trails we have covered so far seem crowded and modern by comparison.

Climbing is hard, going downhill harder. The guides, though comfortable anywhere in these highlands, all prefer going up and it is easy to see why. These trails are rough, jagged, often hardly trails at all. The pack animals churn up loose scree that acts like ball bearings underfoot. Rain carved washouts and gullies create a surface more like a rock-strewn creekbed than a trail. Leigh and I literally watch every step as we descend; carefully planting our trekking poles, carefully plotting each foot placement, practicing defensive hiking to prevent a fall that could prove disastrous. By contrast, Alex seems almost to skip down these slopes. Going our pace, given his skill and natural ability, would clearly be more hazardous for him than going fast.

Today's downhill was grueling, bone-jarring and relentless. Halfway down the mountain I put on my sturdy knee brace, fearful that the increasingly frequent twinges I was feeling might become a sprain. The brace, to my great relief, had the desired effect. My descent became more confident and less painful. The knee brace is here to stay.

We took a brief rest at Pinchiunuyoj, an Inca ruin part way down the mountain. Alex had last seen it a year previously when an ambitious restoration project was in full swing, and he was eager to view the final result. When we arrived at the entrance to the site there was a large sign with details about the project; when it began, when it was completed, how much it cost; some four million Soles. Yet, when we stepped out onto the actual terraces they were already so overgrown with wild squash, tomatoes and brambles that we could barely pass. Though restored less than a year ago, nature is quickly taking the place back. There is no steady flow of visitors to beat down the brush, and no funds have been allotted for maintenance. A few years more and it may disappear entirely into the landscape, waiting to be rediscovered once again.

The last thousand feet down to the Rio Blanco were the worst; steep, treacherous and in full sun. We slipped repeatedly, only saved from injury by our poles and our good fortune. Lunch at the bottom, in the shade by the river, began to restore us. Fifteen minutes of soaking our feet in the icy water completed the job.

Our lunch site on the Rio Blanco was at six thousand feet. Our campsite for the night would be at eleven thousand. Alex told us to expect a five hour climb, an ordeal both Leigh and I had been dreading. We began at 1:15, Leigh setting a moderate and steady pace, me grateful to follow. On the way we saw scores of exotic flowers, some that looked like a whole bouquet in a single blossom. We saw a "walking stick" insect, a favorite from the Disney nature movies of our youth. We see butterflies in delightful, distracting profusion.

The slow ascent took us from the dusty river canyon back up into the cooler, greener cloud forest, a welcome change that lifted our spirits as we lifted our boots. We stopped for short rests often; we loosened our packs and had a snack. We climbed, we talked, and we climbed.

And literally, as if by a miracle, we arrived at our camp. The anticipated five-hour climb had taken us three and a half. Perhaps Alex over estimated a bit. Perhaps our previous days in these mountains have improved our conditioning and our stamina. Whatever the cause, we treated the surprise as a gift from the mountains.

We dropped our gear and caught our breath.

Then we lifted our eyes and gazed out at the rooftop of the world.

Maizal is a compact mountain farm with abundant livestock, a small supply of packed-in provisions for sale, and incomparable views in virtually every direction. Alex says it is his favorite campsite on any trek, anywhere.

We purchased orange Fantas from the woman of the house. We learned that she has a teenaged daughter here on the mountain, and joked that we'd best keep Wilbur busy to keep him out of trouble. Leigh and I sat on the wide grass terrace in front of our tent, and drank our Fantas, and drank it all in.

It is after dinner now, and dark, and I am writing this by headlamp in the quiet of our sleeping tent. The cooks and Domingo and Alex have been joined in the mess tent by the farmer, our host. I listen to them speaking quietly as they share news and sips of Chicha, the corn beer brewed here on the slopes. I hear Alex tell a story that makes them laugh, then another quieter story that makes them listen. Then the farmer begins to speak, his voice low, his Quechua hanging in the air like the clouds that now enfold us. That this is an older story, of the sort told by firesides since the beginning of time, I have no doubt. And though I do not understand a single word, I am sure that in this story there are mountains, extraordinary mountains.

6/5/2010 – SATURDAY –YANAMA
Fourth Camp – 12,540 Feet, 8:30 PM

I just finished a hot cup of "Macho Tea", a savory concoction of black tea, cinnamon and lime, with a liberal portion of Peruvian rum. It is a tradition to toast with Macho Tea at the highest camp on a trek, and tonight, at over twelve thousand feet, will be our highest. It is very cold up here, though zipped into our bags and wearing layers as we deem appropriate we are sure to sleep warm and hard tonight. Leigh could barely wake me for dinner from my after-hike nap; I was so completely gone.

We trekked over the fourteen thousand-foot Victorious Pass today, the highest either of us has ever climbed before. Much of the time we were in the cloud forest. The diversity of the plant life and the feel of this high mountain jungle make this zone a favorite for both of us, in spite of the thick clinging mud on many of these trails. Above the cloud forest we passed into the Puna zone of grasses and open, rocky hillsides. This particular pass is studded with old mining tunnels, many from the Inca times, others that were expanded some hundred and fifty years ago. I explored two with great relish, one in particular that showed the promise of a whole network of shafts and chambers. But I held back, not having either the right equipment or the time to delve deeper.

Our ascent this morning was some three thousand feet and Leigh set a modest, steady pace in deference to the altitude. Slowly, with frequent stops to rest and to marvel at the extraordinary views, we reached the pass. For much of the last thousand feet we were on original Inca road, part of the twenty-four thousand-mile network that united the Inca Empire over five hundred years ago. These trail sections were beautifully laid out, carefully clad with stone treads, and made elegant use of the terrain to gain altitude in the most efficient way possible. Our respect for the accomplishments of the Inca grows with each day.

At lunch, at the very summit of the pass, Domingo cried out, "Condor, Condor!" and one of those magnificent birds went gliding silently overhead. We judged its wingspan to be at least nine feet. Twenty minutes later it graced us with its appearance once again. And moments later, in the distance, a rainbow broke through the clouds.

Our descent after lunch took us past more mine openings, through a zone that felt like a vast rock garden, and into the farming settlement of Yanama. There are no cars here, no roads. Just farms and settlements on either side of the river, marked out by low stone walls, with flocks and crops in great variety everywhere we look. They have a school. They have a single satellite telephone, new last year. They have a lifestyle that is almost impossible to imagine in the twenty-first century.

Tonight we sleep in Yanama, under the Southern Cross and in the soothing embrace of Macho Tea. Tonight, tight in our bags, we sleep.

6/6/2010 – SUNDAY – TATORA
Fifth Camp – 11,979 Feet, 5:12 PM

From where I am sitting as I write this, I look out over our crew as they set up camp, and over the small settlement of Tatora. There is a school and a health clinic, and a store in the two-story mud brick building next to our campsite. There are two little girls playing in the grass near the mess tent. They come up and sit beside me for a moment as I write; all smiles and curiosity. Their father, the proprietor of the store, calls them away before I can attempt to ask their names.

Tatora is a farming community of some thirty families; its boundaries extending up to the fifteen thousand-foot pass we crossed today, our highest ever. As with Yanama yesterday, roads and cars have not yet come this far into the mountains. Electricity for the clinic comes from a generator, silent for the evening. The single telephone is powered by a lone solar panel and batteries, and connects via a satellite dish. We have no idea if it actually works.

We strolled into the settlement a few hours ago, bringing to a close our longest day of trekking at just over thirteen miles. Walking down this valley felt like walking through a landscape painting; flocks grazing on the hillsides, women feeding chickens in their yards and hanging out wash, wranglers leading pack animals over the pass.

The Trek from Yanama started at 7:15 this morning. It is in a valley much like this one, several dozen families calling it home. Our hike toward the pass was mostly on good trail, and took us through large lupine plantations, and past all manner of livestock that often shared the trails with us as we walked. The horsemen and horse-women we encountered cut dashing figures as they passed, and more than one herder actually ran by us to coax wayward stock back into formation. The very idea of running up these trails, at these elevations, is beyond our ability to comprehend. We see it and believe it, but cannot imagine actually doing it.

Our pace as we climbed higher was steady, rhythmic, almost Zen-like; a mantra of footfalls, breaths and pole movements that slowly, slowly got us there. The top was fully bathed in cloud when we arrived. It was raining softly, and a cold wind was at our backs. We took a few minutes to place stone offerings at the summit, as is the local custom for first-timers. We congratulated ourselves, not quite believing that we had managed this. We took shelter in the leeward side of the narrow pass, ate a much-needed snack, and started quickly back down. The climb up had taken us five and a half hours.

Our descent for the first half-hour was miserable. We were in the thinnest air we had ever known. The steady drizzle would not letup; it was cold, it was windy, and the trail was often slick and treacherous with mud.

Yet as we worked our way down to lower elevations all the conditions gradually got better. At fourteen thousand feet we saw the first of many potato fields, the black earth turned by foot plough just as the Quechua did five hundred years ago. The trails improved dramatically, and Alex explained how the locals cooperate to maintain them. There are three ways labor is organized: the work you do for your neighbors, knowing that they will work for you in return, the work you do for your community like improving the mountain trails, and in the time of the Incas, there were the two years of work you were expected to do for the Empire. It is a remarkably simple system, and seems to be serving these mountain people well.

Just now the two little girls from earlier have returned. I am sitting outside as I write this, darkness has fallen, and the light of my headlamp has attracted them. They sit on the embankment just above my shoulder.

I ask their names, and learn that they are Sandra and Melanie. Though I speak and understand almost no Spanish, they manage to tell me that they speak both Spanish and Quechua. I have my digital camera in my pocket, and wanting to engage them in any way that I can, I take a photo of their dog. They are intrigued. I take their picture and they are very pleased. I ask if they attend school, and they both nod. I write out their names and my own in my notebook and show them. They review my efforts with some skepticism, then nod their approval and run off.

They are playing now in the dark, on the grass just a few yards from me. Their squeals mingle with the sounds of the river, and of distant dogs barking in this mist-shrouded Andean night.

6/11/2010 – Friday – 35,000 Feet
7:15 AM, Somewhere over Texas

Our last full day on the remote trail started at 5AM in Totora. It was dark, cold, and stunningly clear; the clouds that had enveloped the valley when we arrived having vanished during the night. We stood in the pre-dawn stillness drinking hot tea, clearing the sleep from our eyes and limbs, and marveling as the moon, stars and slowly rising sun revealed the place to us.

From up the valley, in the direction we had come the night before, a glacier appeared out of the darkness; at first so high and ghostly we assumed it was a mass of clouds clinging to the mountaintops. Then over the hills at our backs a second sliver of white winked into view. And finally ahead of us, impossibly majestic in the brilliant dawn light, the crags and ice pinnacles of Salkantay. All three had been watching over us in our sleep, hidden by the clouds.

This was to be what Alex called our "Break Day," meaning there were no high passes to cross, and less than ten miles to hike to our next camp at Playa. Yet he'd learned from the locals that a recent landslide had closed the regular route. There was a detour, they told him. It only involved going "A little way up". For these mountain Quechua, who sprinted up slopes where we could barely crawl, "A little way", could mean almost anything.

As it happened the detour probably added no more than an hour to our trek, taking us over the sorts of steep, narrow tracks we had, by now, become quite fond of. But as we slowly descended into the valley Alex began to prepare us for a change. A road was pushing its way up the river canyon toward Tatora, a road that would bring with it all that was good and bad about the world outside. A road that would most likely change everything.

When we rounded a bluff and first saw it, a raw, twisting gravel snake freshly hacked into the mountainside, the contrast with where we'd just traveled could not have been starker. A few bewildered cattle stood scattered along its winding course, confused, it seemed, by the feel of crushed gravel beneath their hooves. We soon struck the road ourselves, its grade having obliterated the old mountain path, and this same bewilderment came up to us through our boots.

As quickly as the trails would permit Alex guided us away from the new road and across the river to the still undeveloped side. We trekked once again on winding single tracks that carried us through lush jungle, across precarious mountain-made bridges, and past waterfalls to rival the most beautiful we had ever seen anywhere.

But always, just across the river, there was the new road, cut so improbably into the cliffs that we could scarcely believe it would last a single season. Secretly we hoped that it would not, yet we knew it would. Once it was established, those served by the road would not abide being without its benefits, and would quickly forget that there had ever been a time before it came.

We could not help but debate what the new road meant, the rightness or wrongness of it. Was it even fair for us, mere visitors, to ask these questions? Alex told us that before proceeding the regional government had polled the people who would be affected. Some were opposed, most in favor. It is clearly not for us to question their decision.

We began to see other trekkers from the tail end of the Salkantay loop. They were in bigger groups. They were cleaner than we were. Though we heard them speaking English, it no longer sounded like our language.

Throughout the remotest parts of our trek the few scattered settlements and farms we passed all had makeshift stores, often amounting to no more than a shelf of goods hauled in by pack animals. As we descended further these settlement stores became better stocked, more elaborate, more geared to the larger trekking groups we were starting to see. When we approached one such outpost late in the day, a child came out to solicit our business with a practiced speech and an outstretched hand. This was not a welcome like those we had received in the deep mountains. This was a pitch. No longer viewed as visitors, we had once again become tourists.

Soon a road appeared on our side of the river as well. Not long after that we reached the outskirts of Playa. This looked and felt more like a Mexican border town than an Andean village. We heard our first machine in a week, a chainsaw. We saw our first car. We heard, booming from a shanty, the pounding rhythms of a CD player turned up too loud. The song that greeted us . . . Funky Town.

Playa was swimming with trekkers. Tents were setup almost on top of one another, and the beer stalls were doing a brisk business. Leigh and I were three times older than most of those camped around us.

This was the day that our trekking party would begin to disband. Domingo, with his five pack animals, had to make his way back to his home in Cachora. His path would be much more direct than our outbound trip, and over passes just as steep and treacherous. Yet he would make the journey in three days, and he would do it alone.

We gave Effran six hundred Soles as a thank you gift to the crew. It was his right, as senior man, to distribute this as he saw fit. We were gratified to learn that he divided it evenly among the others. Then we had a simple parting ceremony, and hugged one another, and watched Domingo lead his pack team off into the dusk.

That night after dinner Wilbur served us "Condor Eggs" for desert. These were peach halves in a dish, and looked just like giant egg yokes. Wilbur was quite relieved that his joke went over well, and after the sadness of Domingo's departure we were all glad for the levity.

THE FOLLOWING MORNING after breakfast it was Effran's turn to say goodbye. He would be packing all his gear onto a bus later in the morning and heading for his next trek. He sent us on our way with box lunches of potatoes and rice, and with the modest smile we had come to appreciate from this very modest man.

With no pack animals left to haul our supplies, the duffel bags holding our extra gear now had to be carried, each of them weighting close to twenty pounds. Wilbur assured us he would manage, though we protested that they were far too heavy for him. He insisted and we eventually relented, though only after stuffing our daypacks with as much of the extra weight as they would hold.

Alex then gave us a choice. We could follow the road to the hydro plant and catch the work train into Aguas Calientes, or we could take one last mountain trail over a pass to the Inca ruin of Llactapata, and then down to the train. We jumped at the chance for one last day of real trekking.

Much of the ascent was on old Inca road, and was a delight to travel. We spent hours walking with Wilbur at our sides, he and Leigh alternately practicing their Spanish and English, me attempting the occasional phrase that brought laughter to all of us. And Alex, freed from the need to worry about horses, food and gear, indulged himself with rests in the shade and long visits with the farmers we met along the way. We were, after a week together, four friends out for a hike in countryside we loved.

The beautifully restored ruin of Llactapata was in a mountainside clearing directly across the valley from Mancu Picchu and oriented to face its center perfectly. We ate lunch and explored, and napped a bit on the grass. Finally, reluctantly, we headed down.

At the hydro plant, a huge and growing operation that harnesses the Urubamba River to provide much of the region's electricity, we waited for the work train that would carry laborers home to Aguas Calientes, and trekkers like us to our hostels.

The four of us boarded and took our seats for the slow, steep ride on the old narrow gauge train. We rode in silence, savoring our memories and our fatigue.

When the hive of activity that is Aguas Calientes finally came into view down the track, we pulled our thoughts out of the heavens and prepared to reenter the modern world.

A SOG at Sixty

July 4, 2012 - Kenwood, CA

It is just after 7:30 a.m. and I am less than a mile into the Kenwood 4th of July 10K footrace. It will be hot today, though it's only just hinting at that now. Around me are scores of runners, all experiencing the subtle euphoria that the start of this race always gives. It is early in the morning so you're fresh. Lush shade trees cover most of Warm Springs Road here, so you're cool, and this first mile is ever so slightly downhill. You're at the beginning of a day off, and you are surrounded by hundreds of people who are in pretty good shape and very good spirits.

Your legs and lungs tell you that you could go on like this forever.

They're lying.

Mike Witkowski, a fellow SOG, is running by my side, and we exchange a quick smile. Mike has run as many of these as I have, and we're both aware that the first steep climb is just ahead.

There are just three SOGS – Slow Old Guys - in the race this morning, Mike and myself, and Rory Pool, already minutes ahead. Rory has always been the fastest. Others of us have traded off as slowest in the nearly 20 years that we've been meeting every Sunday morning in the lane out in front of Rory and Deb's house. The SOGS have never been about speed. We run together, usually a handful of us, always with conversation to carry us along.

Up ahead the course swings right onto Lawndale Road and everything changes as we hit the first hill. Some runners beside us turn into walkers and slip from view. Others dig in and attack, actually picking up speed. Mike and I search for a lower gear, find it, and take the hill steadily together as the faces and paces shift all around us. We crest the hill and the river of runners carries us forward between green banks of vineyard on either side; a current of color, movement, and welcome toil.

We met when our kids were in elementary school. We had that, our age, and the little town of Glen Ellen in common, but not much else. Leigh was a doctor from New England, Mike a surfer from San Diego turned 4th grade teacher. Chuck worked as a phone company line-man, Ritch as a contractor, Bruce as a high school math and science teacher. Matt was a park ranger, Rory an arborist, and I managed a small manufacturing business. Some of us had played high school sports, a few had competed in college, but none of us were really jocks. We were just guys who had picked up the running habit and somehow managed to find each other on a Sunday morning back when we were all a lot younger.

The Kenwood 10K has three hills that count. Mike and I are past the first one, and though I'm feeling pretty good I can tell from Mike's breathing that he's working hard. We've all been there. I can see the next hill just ahead, and wonder which of us will start a story first. A good yarn can't get you up a hill all by itself, but it can sure help, particularly if you're the one spinning it.

I've got one in mind, but before I can begin Mike launches into his, about a guy he met on a tramp steamer back in his college days. Good, I'm thinking, this will get us there. We hit the incline and both of us alter our pace, looking for that elusive better gear. I find mine but today Mike doesn't; sometimes you just don't. I have probably walked this hill more than I've run it over the years, but today won't be one of those times. Mike and I will meet up at the finish.

We SOGS almost never run for times. It isn't that we ignore them, and posting a good one is always personally satisfying, but the running itself is really the goal. All of us have flirted with losing the ability to do this, through inaction or injury. Eleven years ago we lost Bruce to a heart attack. It wasn't a wake up call so much as a reminder; if we can do this thing that we love we should keep doing it for as long as we can. We've got good friends who can't imagine running unless some-one is chasing them. We can't imagine not running; it's that simple.

I crest the second hill and take stock. The slight groin pull I felt getting out of bed this morning seems to be behaving. My right shoulder has mostly recovered from the spill I took two weeks ago, and my left knee has settled down after the overworking I gave it last month.

We are past the worst climb, over the summit, and well into the long downhill glide that will take us back to the valley floor. Some runners who went sprinting past me on the steeper downgrade are virtually spent now; and still we have a mile and a half to go.

I see one such fellow up ahead, walking fast and panting with each stride. He's about my size and in his mid-forties I'd guess. As I run past he can't help but read the SOG running strategy on the back of my shirt, "Start out slow, then let up." Being passed by a Slow Old Guy does not sit well, and soon he is panting past me again.

The first time you run Kenwood the third hill appears like an insult thrown in your face. You're on level ground, the finish is on level ground, why would there be a hill between the two? But there it is, and I approach it now with the respect of an old adversary. We are running through private property here, made even more beautiful by the fact that it is seldom seen. The vineyard road tilts upward. I reach for a lower gear, am relieved to find one, and know for the first time since starting this morning that today I won't be walking until I cross the finish line.

There are as many reasons to run as there are runners. I think the SOGS do it because the regularity of our Sunday outings creates a rhythm, like footfalls across the calendar pages of our years. Our strides may lengthen or shorten, but once a week we can count on our feet all coming down together.

That and Ibuprofen keeps us going.

I am coming off the final hill now. For the last several minutes the panting guy has been surging past me, walking until I pull a few yards ahead, then surging and panting past again.

He is determined not to be beaten by a SOG.

We round the final turn back onto Warm Springs Road and I can see the finish line a half-mile in the distance. I stride steadily past the panting guy and a few seconds later hear him coming on again, a locomotive of exhaustion; too much couch time and not enough trail time, but absolutely no intention of slacking off.

Imperceptibly I quicken my pace. He is still approaching, though closing the gap more slowly now. He will pass me before the finish if I hold my present speed, no doubt about it.

Twenty years ago I would have kicked this final quarter mile, going all out regardless of the cost; my own version of the panting guy. Those days are long gone, and a good thing, too.

All the same I might have a little something left, just to make it interesting.

I take stock one final time.

And find, to my delight, that everything is still working.

The Place That We Come Back To

This is where we live.

No two of us see its textures with the same eyes, hear its rhythms with the same clarity, or feel its happiness, heartbreak and hope with the same intensity, yet we each do know it and no one knows it better.

This is where we live.

As many of us came to this place as left someplace else, but whether we landed here by design, destiny or default something about it has made us stick. We may be held by the closeness of a friend or a lover, by the anchor of family and the past, or because we like it, love it, or have simply gotten used to it. Some fought hard to get here, and struggle constantly just to stay. Others, here from birth, may never have known anywhere else. But few, if any, are anxious to leave.

This is where we live.

We do not know everyone we see on the street, and most of them do not know us, but we are familiar to each other in a way that makes us something less than friends but considerably more than strangers. Our closest neighbors often seem entirely obscure to us, and we honor their anonymity as much as we value our own. Yet we do notice their lives going on around us, and we're mostly grateful that they notice ours.

This is where we live.

And this is where our friends live. We don't necessarily have a lot of them, we don't necessarily see them every day, but they're here, and they're close, and we feel better for it. The times we look forward to are often spent with them, and they're just as often in the times we remember. We laugh with them, and worry, and willingly mingle our tears and triumphs and pains with theirs. We have other friends in other places, friends we love as much and miss even more. They are the friends we tell our lives to. These are the friends we live our lives with.

This is where we live.

And it's just the way we like it, just the way it's always been, but it isn't, and we know that, and we wish it wasn't so. We don't resist change as much as regret it, and if we could turn the clock back many of us would, back to the very moment we arrived. We remember what the air felt like then, how the sounds were clearer and the colors brighter, and the way a simple evening breeze could sometimes break your heart. We remember it, and miss it, until one morning we open our old eyes to a new day and realize that it's all still here and always has been. The only things that no longer change are those things that no longer live, and this place is very much alive.

This is where we live.

It's where our children grow, and our work gets done, and our evenings pass with our lovers in our arms. It's the place that we come back to and the place that we lose people from. And each of us understands, in a way that we seldom acknowledge but can never deny, that this place would not be the same without us, and we would not be the same without it.

This is where we live.

This is home.

Made in the USA
Lexington, KY
22 February 2018